Maritime Piracy

Maritime piracy is now a pressing global issue, and this work seeks to provide a concise and informative introduction to the area. Never truly having receded into a romanticized past, seaborne banditry's rapid growth was stimulated by low risks and increasingly high rewards. Currently, obsolete, incomplete and complicating structures and norms of governance, together with advances in technology, enable a lucrative business model for pirates, as they effectively operate with impunity and claim increasing ransoms.

Beginning with an overview and historical development of piracy and the relevant maritime governance structures, this work progresses to examine how twentieth-century shifts in global governance norms and structures eventually left the high seas open for predatory attacks on one of the world's fastest growing and essential industries. Moving through contemporary debates about how to best combat piracy, the work concludes that the solution to a chronic global problem requires a long-term, holistic, and inclusive approach.

Examining militaristic, legal, and humanitarian strategies and offering a critical evaluation of the various problems they bring, this work will be of great interest to all students and scholars of international law, international organizations, and maritime security.

Robert Haywood is Senior Fellow at One Earth Future Foundation

Roberta Spivak is a Researcher at One Earth Future Foundation

Routledge Global Institutions Series

Edited by Thomas G. Weiss
The CUNY Graduate Center, New York, USA
and Rorden Wilkinson
University of Manchester, UK

About the series

The Global Institutions Series is designed to provide readers with comprehensive, accessible, and informative guides to the history, structure, and activities of key international organizations as well as books that deal with topics of key importance in contemporary global governance. Every volume stands on its own as a thorough and insightful treatment of a particular topic, but the series as a whole contributes to a coherent and complementary portrait of the phenomenon of global institutions at the dawn of the millennium.

Books are written by recognized experts, conform to a similar structure, and cover a range of themes and debates common to the series. These areas of shared concern include the general purpose and rationale for organizations, developments over time, membership, structure, decision-making procedures, and key functions. Moreover, current debates are placed in historical perspective alongside informed analysis and critique. Each book also contains an annotated bibliography and guide to electronic information as well as any annexes appropriate to the subject matter at hand.

The volumes currently published are:

63 Maritime Piracy (2012)
by Robert Haywood (One Earth Future) and Roberta Spivak (One Earth Future)

62 United Nations High Commissioner for Refugees (UNHCR) (2nd edition, 2012)
by Gil Loescher (University of Oxford), Alexander Betts (University of Oxford), and James Milner (University of Toronto)

Books currently under contract include:

The Changing Political Map of Global Governance
*by Anthony Payne (University of Sheffield) and Stephen Robert
Buzdugan (Manchester Metropolitan University)*

Decolonization, Sovereignty, and the African Union
by Martin Welz (University of Konstanz)

Feminist Strategies in International Governance
*edited by Gülay Caglar (Humboldt University of Berlin), Elisabeth
Prügl (Graduate Institute of International and Development
Studies, Geneva), Susanne Zwingel (SUNY Potsdam)*

Private Foundations and Development Partnerships
by Michael Moran (Swinburne University of Technology)

For further information regarding the series, please contact:

Craig Fowlie, Senior Publisher, Politics & International Studies
Taylor & Francis
2 Park Square, Milton Park, Abingdon
Oxford OX14 4RN, UK
+44 (0)207 842 2057 Tel
+44 (0)207 842 2302 Fax
Craig.Fowlie@tandf.co.uk
www.routledge.com

Maritime Piracy

Robert Haywood and Roberta Spivak

Routledge
Taylor & Francis Group

LONDON AND NEW YORK

First published 2012
by Routledge
2 Park Square, Milton Park, Abingdon, Oxon, OX14 4RN

Simultaneously published in the USA and Canada
by Routledge
711 Third Avenue, New York, NY 10017

Routledge is an imprint of the Taylor & Francis Group, an informa business

© 2012 Robert Haywood and Roberta Spivak

British Library Cataloguing in Publication Data
A catalogue record for this book is available from the British Library

Library of Congress Cataloging in Publication Data
Haywood, Robert.
  Maritime piracy / Robert Haywood and Roberta Spivak.
    p. cm. – (Global institutions)
  Includes bibliographical references and index.
  1. Piracy–Prevention–International cooperation. 2. Hijacking of ships–
Prevention–International cooperation. 3. Maritime terrorism–Prevention–
International cooperation. 4. Merchant marine–Security measures. 5.
Shipping–Security measures. I. Spivak, Roberta. II. Title.
  HV6433.785.H39 2012
  364.16'4–dc23   **1006673095**
        2011042090

ISBN13: 978-0-415-78197-8 (hbk)
ISBN13: 978-0-415-78198-5 (pbk)
ISBN13: 978-0-203-14481-7(ebk)

Typeset in Times New Roman
by Taylor & Francis Books

MIX
Paper from
responsible sources
FSC
www.fsc.org FSC® C004839

Printed and bound in Great Britain by
TJ International Ltd, Padstow, Cornwall

To Erin Jellel Collins Arsenault, who taught us so much about the need for a world beyond war.

Contents

Illustrations

Figures

Tables

Foreword

The current volume is the sixty-third title in a dynamic series on global institutions. These books provide readers with definitive guides to the most visible aspects of what many of us know as "global governance." Remarkable as it may seem, there exist relatively few books that offer in-depth treatments of prominent global bodies, processes, and associated issues, much less an entire series of concise and complementary volumes. Those that do exist are either out of date, inaccessible to the non-specialist reader, or seek to develop a specialized understanding of particular aspects of an institution or process rather than offer an overall account of its functioning and situate it within the increasingly dense global institutional network. Similarly, existing books have often been written in highly technical language or have been crafted "in-house" and are notoriously self-serving and narrow.

The advent of electronic media has undoubtedly helped research and teaching by making data and primary documents of international organizations more widely available, but it has complicated matters as well. The growing reliance on the Internet and other electronic methods of finding information about key international organizations and processes has served, ironically, to limit the educational and analytical materials to which most readers have ready access—namely, books. Public relations documents, raw data, and loosely refereed web sites do not make for intelligent analysis. Official publications compete with a vast amount of electronically available information, much of which is suspect because of its ideological or self-promoting slant. Paradoxically, a growing range of purportedly independent web sites offering analyses of the activities of particular organizations has emerged, but one inadvertent consequence has been to frustrate access to basic, authoritative, readable, critical, and well-researched texts. The market for such has actually been reduced by the ready availability of varying quality electronic materials.

For those of us who teach, research, and operate in the area, such restricted access to information and analyses has been frustrating. We were delighted when Routledge saw the value of a series that bucks this trend and provides key reference points to the most significant global institutions and issues. They are betting that serious students and professionals will want serious analyses. We have assembled a first-rate team of authors to address that market. Our intention is to provide one-stop shopping for all readers—students (both undergraduate and postgraduate), negotiators, diplomats, practitioners from nongovernmental and intergovernmental organizations, and interested parties alike—seeking insights into the most prominent institutional aspects of global governance.

Maritime Piracy

When we conceived this series in 2005, certain titles seemed necessities, but we were not prescient enough to foresee the importance of the return of an old blight on the international agenda, namely the re-emergence of piracy on the high seas. Maritime piracy was thrust back into the public's and media's attention by highly visible and publicized hijackings off the coast of Somalia.

In the age of nuclear weapons and sophisticated drones attacking belligerents, how could a tiny group of men in small boats equipped with machine guns pose a significant—the authors claim that the total bill could approach $12 billion per year—problem to international shipping? The answer is akin to that for many books in this series, namely that piracy takes place outside the actual jurisdiction of any state but causes damage to all. The world may be increasingly interconnected, but public international law and international organizations still reflect the fundamental building blocks of state sovereignty. And states are unwilling or unable to live up to their historical and treaty-based obligations to prevent piracy.

Piracy—like terrorism or climate change or pandemics—is a global threat that requires new approaches, laws, and organizations to tackle the problems posed by increasingly global, but disjointed, arrangements for global governance.

We were delighted when Bob Haywood and Roberta Spivak agreed to take up the challenge of writing about this problem for this series. Both have been involved in conceiving and carrying out a multinational and multidisciplinary research project over the last two years conducted by One Earth Future. Both Bob and Roberta have practical experience in the field and in headquarters of governmental, intergovernmental, and nongovernmental organizations but also bring to bear a critical analytical eye to this long-ignored subject. More importantly, they have also brought to bear the policy insights from one of the few research efforts working on this challenge.

As always, we welcome comments and suggestions from our readers.

Thomas G. Weiss, The CUNY Graduate Center,
New York, USA
Rorden Wilkinson, University of Manchester, UK
July 2011

Acknowledgments

We would like to thank One Earth Future (OEF) for the support they provided in the writing of *Maritime Piracy*. OEF was founded by Marcel Arsenault with a goal of a "world beyond war" within one hundred years. OEF believes that a peaceful world is achievable through more effective and inclusive governance structures that will bring states, civil society organizations, commercial enterprises, and intergovernmental organizations together on an equal basis to develop more effective policies on an issue-specific basis. OEF's flagship project, Oceans Beyond Piracy, was launched in 2010 because it was already clear that there was no effective governance plan for suppressing piracy. The project is engaging various stakeholders in governments, industry, and civil society to help coordinate an effective consensus-based solution.

We very much appreciate Thomas G. Weiss and Rorden Wilkinson for asking us to write this book and providing us with a very insightful critique of our draft manuscript. Martin Burke, Nicola Parkin and Megan Graieg kindly guided us through the editorial process. Marcel Arsenault's faith and enthusiasm for this project was important in sustaining our efforts.

We would like to give specific acknowledgment to Conor Seyle who rolled up his sleeves at critical moments, providing us not only with sage counsel but supplying content as we approached the due date. We are grateful to our colleagues at OEF, several of whom read the manuscript from cover to cover and whose insights and opinions strengthened every page: Andrew Lee, Anna Bowden, Bronwyn Bruton, Charles Nicholas, Chris Hall, Eamon Aloyo, Jeffrey French, Jens Vestergaard Madsen, Jon Huggins, Kasey Pennington, Kaija Hurlburt, Mani Chandy, Maisie Pigeon, Martin Murphy, Michael Pemberton, Meadow Didier, Peter Nordby, Theodore Langan, Tracie Ware, and the many interns who worked hard at OEF but are too numerous to name individually.

Dan Klein and Maurice Janssen graciously provided us with all the resources we required to focus on our research. Diane Alfrey was a lifeline in so many ways. She made us laugh at the more stressful moments and offered much-needed advice throughout.

Robert Haywood would like to specifically thank Barbara Cole who not only provided a quiet place to work, but also through it all gave freely of her time, intellect, and wit.

Roberta Spivak would like to thank Bill Gotthelf and Ben and Rachel who had tremendous patience with a largely absent mother. Much to their chagrin, takeout dinners will soon be a thing of the past. Sam and Lorraine Spivak offered continuous encouragement, as always.

As much as this book was a team effort, the authors are responsible for any errors throughout.

Abbreviations

BIMCO	Baltic and International Maritime Council
BMP	Best management practices
CAT	Convention Against Torture
Contact Group	Contact Group on Piracy off the Coast of Somalia
Combined Task	CTF-151
Djibouti Code	Djibouti Code of Conduct Concerning the Repression of Piracy and Armed Robbery Against Ships in the Region
ECHR	European Convention on Human Rights
EEZ	Exclusive Economic Zone
EU	European Union
ICC	International Criminal Court
ICCPR	International Convention on Civil and Political Rights
ITF	International Transport Workers Federation
IMB	International Maritime Bureau
IMO	International Maritime Organization
INTERTANKO	International Association of Independent Tank Owners
ISPS	International Ship and Port Facility Security Code
ITLOS	International Tribunal of the Law of the Sea
MoU	Memorandum of Understanding
MOWCA	Maritime Organization of West and Central Africa
NATO	North Atlantic Treaty Organization
NGO	Nongovernmental organization
ReCAAP	The Regional Cooperation Agreement on Combating Piracy and Armed Robbery Against Ships in Asia
ReCAAP ISC	ReCAAP Information Sharing Center
SAMI	Security Association for the Maritime Industry

SHADE	Shared Awareness and De-confliction
SOLAS	Safety of Life at Sea Convention
SUA	Suppression of Unlawful Acts Against the Safety of Maritime Navigation
TFG	Transitional Federal Government
UDHR	Universal Declaration on Human Rights
UKMTO	United Kingdom Maritime Trade Operations
UN	United Nations
UNCLOS	United Nations Convention on the Law of the Sea
UNDP	United Nations Development Program
UNODC	United Nations Office on Drugs and Crime
UNSCR	United Nations Security Council Resolution
VLCC	Very Large Crude Carrier

Introduction

Maritime piracy was thrust into the public eye by three extraordinary hijackings off the coast of Somalia. The first occurred in September 2008 when a group of Somali pirates captured the MV Faina with its cargo of 33 Russian-made T-72 battle tanks and a large assortment of arms and ammunition. Then seven weeks later on 15 November another group of Somali pirates hijacked the 1,089 ft. (332 m) MV Sirius Star, a very large crude carrier (VLCC) laden with over two million barrels of crude oil. The third event was the hijacking of the MV Maersk Alabama in April 2009, which resulted in a dramatic hostage situation, including US military operations to release the ship and rescue the captain, Richard Philips. Although these incidents received both public and official attention as new developments, the maritime industry knew that Somali piracy—alongside piracy throughout the world—had been going on for decades. In 2010 alone there were 191 piracy-related incidents off the coast of Somalia, resulting in 53 hijacked ships, with 1,090 seafarers on board.[1] There were at least 70 pirate attacks in Southeast Asia in that year and Nigeria experienced over 293 pirate attacks between 2003 and 2008.[2]

One should wonder how this is possible. In an age of aircraft carriers and guided missile frigates, where maritime powers have the capacity to place enormous naval strength at nearly any point across the seas, why is it that small groups of armed men in rickety skiffs can pose a significant problem to maritime shipping? In part the answer lies in the fact that piracy often takes place outside the jurisdiction of any state—in what many refer to as "the global commons." The world is increasingly globalized, while international law and international engagements are still built around the state as the fundamental source of legal action. Yet many states have either lost the capacity to live up to their historical and treaty-based obligations to prevent piracy or are not willing to do so. The current international system has not yet adapted to this state deficiency and organized an alternative global governance structure to define who has the obligation or authority to fill these gaps. Piracy is a global challenge that requires the creation of organizations and new legal structures to tackle the problems posed by an increasingly global, but disjointed, governance environment.

Another impediment to tackling privacy is that the international relations system of the twenty-first century is vastly different from systems of previous eras, yet it still relies on the laws and customs from those previous times. And while ancient laws and customs have periodically worked to suppress ancient manifestations of piracy, they have proven insufficient in the modern world. We explore these gaps on the local and global level because in one sense piracy is a global problem—it occurs throughout the world and affects people and goods of many states. It is also subject to international treaties and norms that define piracy and both empower and limit states' responses to suppress it. But conversely piracy is also a local problem, rooted firmly in the specific conditions that allowed its emergence. One needs only to look at the vastly different manifestations of piracy in three "hot-spots"—Somalia, Nigeria, and the Strait of Malacca to see the importance of local drivers and governance.

In order to address these issues we examine several related questions including:

What is piracy, and who has the authority to define it?

How have states managed piracy throughout history, and how does prior management affect the way we manage piracy in the twenty-first century?

What are the systems in place for managing piracy and how effective are they?

What has changed from past eras of piracy that might affect piracy management systems, and what systems could develop to respond to these changes?

Does the current system adequately protect seafarers?

How can we do better?

Suppressing piracy requires that potential pirates not be exposed to low-risk, high-reward incentives that lure them into the practice. Strategies to accomplish that end consist of creating both high legal and personal risks for engaging in piracy and an environment in which alternative actions are more attractive. Yet these strategies can be difficult to implement in a world where poverty and poor governance are still abundant.

A return to past centuries' reliance on military force to hunt pirates on land and sea runs aground when wading into twenty-first century norms of human rights and sovereignty. In *Maritime Piracy*, we map out the development of these dynamics and the interplay among them. Beginning with an overview in Chapter 1, we briefly present the scope of the problem, defining piracy and the general ways that states have viewed pirates throughout the centuries. We go on to analyze its many costs to people, the environment, and business society. Our intention is not only to give an understanding of piracy throughout the ages but to dispel several common misperceptions—namely that piracy is a "Somalia problem" or that piracy ceased to be relevant by the mid nineteenth century. Rather we argue that piracy has continually plagued ungoverned areas and that Somalia is only one of several hot spots of piracy around the globe.

We then examine the history of piracy in Chapter 2. We explore states' fickle attitude toward pirates, highlighting that states did not always view pirates as enemies. In fact they often allied with pirates to achieve specific strategic objectives. Once these objectives were met or when pirates were seen as interfering with state welfare, rulers responded with both general amnesties and overwhelming military might. We also examine several themes in the history of piracy, including the importance of the state of ship registry—the flag state—and how changes in the nature of flag states have diminished the states' capacity to protect their ships at the same time that their legal responsibilities were enhanced by international conventions. We also look at the dichotomy of public perceptions of pirates: they were just as likely to be feared and reviled as honored for their bravery and independence from what were often brutal social structures.

In Chapter 3 we discuss the "nuts and bolts" of twenty-first century counterpiracy efforts coming from government, business, and civil society that are part of a complex, well-established framework to suppress piracy. These stakeholders realize that cooperation is the key to bringing down levels of piracy and billions of dollars are being spent annually to accomplish this task.[3] Yet the system, which is impressive in many ways, has accomplished little in its counterpiracy work. Chapter 3 offers some reasons why these organizations may not have achieved much success.

Chapter 4 analyzes how evolving norms have changed the way modern states counter pirates. It discusses the idea of human rights, the basic premise of which is that a person who commits unjust acts is equally entitled to human rights as the law-abiding citizen. Changes in human rights norms have stripped away the older notion that pirates "are enemies of all" meriting the protection of none. It describes the human rights treaties and conventions that modern navies and judiciaries are bound by when confronting pirates. The second norm we discuss concerns territoriality. States no longer feel entitled to "carve up" the sea to suit their own purposes as they had in past centuries. By the twenty-first century the sea was considered the common heritage of all and not a protectorate of some. This chapter also tackles the issue of sovereignty and how changing notions of sovereignty hamper international counterpiracy efforts. Finally, Chapter 4 describes the codification of these changing norms in international law and convention, most notably in the United Nations Convention on the Law of the Sea (UNCLOS).

The changing nature of how states should counter pirates has catalyzed many debates. In Chapter 5 we address these debates, focusing on the legal, tactical, and philosophical arguments about how to engage with pirates. The chapter examines both sides of contentious philosophical issues such as whether pirates should be considered terrorists and whether military strikes on pirates' home bases are the answer to shutting down the pirate enterprise. It continues with a more technical examination of legal disputes such as whether transferring suspected pirates to third-party states for trial is legal. Chapter 5 closes with a look at the more tactical debates in piracy circles, namely, whether shippers should hire armed security guards and pay ransoms to free their crews after they have been taken hostage.

Chapter 6 examines the gaps in the system that allow piracy to emerge. It highlights the failure of some coastal states as the first line of defense to prevent pirates from operating from their shores. When the coastal state fails to deter pirates there is no longer a second line of defense as there was in previous eras when the flag state had the capacity and interest to protect its merchants. The failures of these two traditional lines of defense are the main gaps in preventing piracy epidemics but other gaps in the system exacerbate the challenge of counterpiracy work. Gaps in legal mechanisms and naval capacity to patrol volatile coasts are some of these, but knowledge limitations on such issues as how to fix failed states are also serious concerns.

Moving through contemporary debates about how to best combat piracy, we conclude in Chapter 7 by noting that the solution to a chronic global problem requires a long-term, holistic, and inclusive approach. Countering piracy requires global governance structures because the crime often occurs in the global commons—that is, outside the territory of any state. Conquering piracy fundamentally challenges our current notions of a state-centered international system. It prods us to go beyond this system and to develop new ways for states, individuals, and organizations to work together to solve shared problems occurring on the global commons.

The purpose of this book is not necessarily to present a comprehensive plan for the solution of piracy, but to explore three main ideas: 1) that piracy results from a lack of effective governance (globally and locally); 2) that ancient customs and laws which provide the framework for counterpiracy measure are inconsistent with modern realities; and 3) that new systems of governance that account for modern realities must be evaluated and implemented.

1 Piracy
The nature of the problem

- **What is piracy and what are pirates?**
- **Modern piracy**
- **Costs of piracy**
- **Conclusion**

When maritime piracy resurfaced as a front-page story, many readers greeted it with surprise and even derision. By the end of the twentieth century, piracy in the popular imagination was a romantic relic of the past, a view that had been the perception of the academic world for over a century. In an article on the law of piracy, published in 1874, A. T. Whatley remarked that there seemed "very little occasion for such a law."[1] Although the shipping industry and those who ventured out to sea knew differently, most people believed that piracy had been stamped out in centuries past. But by the beginning of the twenty-first century, this notion was quickly disproven and modern piracy—violent, and often brutal—had roared back to life off the Horn of Africa, in the Strait of Malacca in Southeast Asia, and in the Gulf of Guinea off the coast of Nigeria. By 2011 it was a fact of modern life costing the global economy between $7 billion and $12 billion annually.[2] Its toll was not only economic but human and "in the first three months of 2011 alone, pirates murdered seven seafarers and injured 34."[3] In truth, piracy never did recede into a romanticized past. It has continually existed, "albeit on a low, sporadic, and opportunistic level, in some backwaters of the world's oceans" from ancient times forward.[4]

This book attempts to explore the many facets of piracy that allow it to flourish in the modern world, from the new multinational face of global shipping to the evolving norms that affect potential solutions. As a first step, it is important to give a general overview of piracy, dispel the many misconceptions surrounding it, and address the basic questions: (1) what is piracy; (2) how does it operate in the modern world; and (3) what are the costs of piracy to society, local politics, and the environment?

What is piracy, and what are pirates?

Perhaps the most difficult question to answer is the most basic. What is piracy? The great historian Plutarch writing about 100 CE gave perhaps the oldest clear definition. He described pirates as those who attacked on sea and coastal land without legal authority. Plutarch's definition gives us an early indication that it was not the behavior of the seaborne robbers that defined them as pirates but rather their relation with the existing authorities. Modern states' relations with pirates are less complicated. States do not give pirates legal authority to rob others at sea or coastal land and therefore piracy is never seen as acceptable. States now view piracy as "predatory maritime activities"[5] undertaken for personal (not political) gain. This was not always the case. As implied by Plutarch, states have taken different approaches to pirates historically. States' views of pirates have historically fallen into three broad categories. They saw them as potential allies, enemies, or criminals. The distinction between allies and enemies reflects whether pirates were aiding or obstructing state interests. The distinction between labeling pirates as enemies or criminals reflected the changing opinion on how to treat them.

In the ancient world states considered pirates who worked against them as enemies who were in a perpetual state of war against the world. Yet by the early modern era, states began to view pirates as criminals to be dealt with by judicial means. This change in perception had to do in part with the development of legal norms and with the economic costs resulting from the instability of war.

Each perspective makes certain assumed demands on society to deal with the piracy in a particular way. If pirates are defined as criminals, then they are owed the same treatment as any other civilian criminal, including in most modern states due process under a fair and humane criminal justice system. If states define pirates as combatants or even privateers representing a sovereign, then the quite different "rules of war" apply. For example, a state may use lethal force against a combatant, or hold a combatant as a prisoner of war until the end of hostilities without the rules and requirements of evidence and judicial process that would be required by a criminal justice system.

The ancient, and until relatively recently the most common, approach to pirates was to view oceangoing robbers as enemy combatants engaged in military attacks against the state and its constituents.

Ancient Romans used the term *"hostis"* or "enemy" rather than a word to denote a criminal to describe pirates. Although often given credit for it, Cicero never called pirates *"hostis humani generis"* or "enemies of all mankind," but rather *"communis hostis omnium"* which means that pirates are "communities against all."[6] In Cicero's interpretation pirates were not just individual seafarers engaged in robbery and depredation, but communities engaged in a war against all. The distinction is important because from the state's perspective, Rome did not have to declare war against pirates—they were already engaged in a perpetual war against them.[7] Pirates themselves responded to the states' condemnation. In a famous story from Greek history, Alexander the Great asked a captured pirate "how he dares molest the sea." The pirate replied, "How dare you molest the whole world? Because I do it with a little ship only, I am called a thief; you, doing it with a great navy, are called an Emperor."[8]

Viewing pirates as combatants to be engaged with military force, has persisted throughout history. President Thomas Jefferson of the United States did not send the US Navy to Tripoli in 1802 to arrest Yusuf Karamanli, the Bey of Tripoli, but to seize all vessels and goods of the Bey of Tripoli and his subjects. Congress never voted on a formal declaration of war, but did pass a resolution that the President was "to cause to be done all such other acts of precaution or hostility as the state of war will justify."[9] However, as will be discussed later, changes in international law and human rights norms gradually made this approach to piracy less favored, and by the twentieth century it was not generally seen as an appropriate framing for piracy by Western states.

While ancient regimes generally regarded pirates as engaging in war, by the early modern era European sovereigns often sought out seafarers to engage in piratical acts on their behalf. "Privateering" as this practice was called, provided a less expensive way for nations to supplement their naval forces, and until the nineteenth century was a common activity. The English, Dutch, French, Venetians, Ottomans, Spanish, and Portuguese, among many others, all commissioned privateers, and there was an internationally recognized set of rules for privateers.[10,11] Sailing under letters of marque, which gave them license to attack the enemies of the state, privateers worked for two causes at the same time—their own enrichment and the military aims of their sponsors. During the brief war of 1812, the United States issued more than five hundred letters of marque to privateers, who captured or sank more than seventeen hundred British ships.[12] It was a time when "national and individual interests could be pursued in tandem, and a fortune could be won while ostensibly serving the state."[13] Privateering was difficult to control, however, and in 1856 the major powers of Europe, excluding Spain, declared in the Declaration Respecting Maritime Law that "Privateering is, and remains, abolished."[14] The United States was not a signatory in 1856, but in 1907 it was party to the Hague Convention, which also banned privateering, although permitted private vessels to be used in time of war as warships if under the command of a naval officer.

Nevertheless, privateering is not necessarily a relic of history. Jardine Lloyd Thompson Group is proposing a "Convoy Escort Program," to deal with Somali piracy in which they would develop a nonprofit company that would outfit a small number of armed patrol boats to escort ships in the Gulf of Aden. It is claimed that the scheme would be classed as a "flag naval company" under the maritime and criminal law of a still-to-be-decided flag state.[15] Whether this arrangement—essentially licensing private citizens to engage in naval action against enemies of the state—will be seen as privateering, and how the signers of the Treaty of Paris or the Hague Convention will reconcile their citizens and companies being involved in such an operation are yet to be understood.

In general, however, states in the twenty-first century do not view pirates as enemies or allies but rather as criminals. As such they treat pirates with the tools and structures of the criminal justice system and not with the military force deployed against combatants. This new classification began with the legal writings of Italian jurist Alberico Gentili in the late sixteenth century, who linked the criminality of piracy to state sovereignty. In his writing, piracy committed under the authority of the state (as in privateering) was legal, while that done without such authority was illegal. The march to criminalization was also prompted by the evolution of ethical considerations, relevant to the perceptions of appropriate behavior in war. In earlier ages the prevailing view, as expressed by Thucydides speaking in the fifth century BCE, was that "to a king or commonwealth, nothing is unjust which is useful."[16] By the seventeenth century CE jurists began to advance a different notion—that even in war states should abide by certain laws to regulate conduct. One of the first codifications of this idea came from the Swedish king Gustavus Adolphus in 1618. The 167 entries in his Articles of War outlined legal behavior of soldiers in war. According to legal scholars Richard J. Goldstone and Adam M. Smith, these articles eventually led to the Hague and Geneva conventions that created the rules of war and the concept of war crimes and its corollary, international humanitarian law.[17] If pirates were not military personnel as established in these conventions or otherwise under the jurisdiction of these conventions, then they must by default be subject to the proper civilian judicial process.

By the twentieth century, the global consensus was that those who commit predatory acts on the sea should be considered criminals. With the larger issue solved, legal scholars turned their attention to codifying the law. How to define piracy was a challenge that proved more difficult than many would have imagined. In 1932, the members of the Harvard Research in International Law project wrote about the inherent difficulties in coming up with a legal definition:

> An investigation finds that instead of a single relatively simple problem, there are a series of difficult problems which have occasioned a great diversity of professional opinion. In studying the content of the (definition) article, it is useful to bear in mind the chaos of expert opinion as to what the law of nations includes, or should include, in piracy. There is no authoritative definition. Of the many definitions that have been proposed, most are inaccurate, both as to what they literally include and as to what they omit. Some are impromptu, rough descriptions of a typical piracy.[18]

The consequences of their inability to formulate a satisfying definition are discussed more in Chapter 6. For now it is important to note that the most authoritative legal definition of piracy can be found in the United Nations Convention on the Law of the Sea (UNCLOS) starting with Article 100. It is based almost entirely on the work of the Harvard Draft Convention and it defines piracy as having four elements: (1) piracy is "any illegal acts of violence or detention or depredation"[19] at sea; (2) there must be two vessels involved (mutiny is not piracy); (3) the illegal act must be committed on the high seas—"outside the jurisdiction of any state"[19]; and (4) its aim must be for private and not political ends. It also declares "inciting or intentionally facilitating" an act of piracy is equivalent to piracy.[21]

UNCLOS also makes clear what is *not* defined as piracy under the treaty. According to UNCLOS any action committed by a state is not considered piracy. So, for instance, no matter what one may think of the May 2010 Israeli raid of the Gaza flotilla—a legitimate action of self-defense or a murderous attack on civilians—the fact is that according to international convention the Israeli action does not constitute piracy as some have suggested.[22] Armed robberies occurring within the inland water or territorial seas of a state are also not defined as piracy according to UNCLOS. This makes it possible for Nigeria to claim that there is no piracy in Nigeria.[23] For those seafarers harmed in territorial waters this is a "distinction without a difference."[24] There is rampant robbery and murder of fishermen and passengers on Lake Victoria, which is bordered by Kenya, Uganda, and Tanzania, but it is not acknowledged as piracy under local laws or international convention[25] because it occurs entirely on inland waters. UNCLOS does not prohibit states from defining acts of piracy within their interior waters and territorial seas, and some have, but many have not. The individual state definitions do not have to be consistent with UNCLOS. For example, contrary to the UNCLOS definition, current US law declares that a shore raid from a pirate vessel or by the crew of a pirate vessel is piracy.[26]

In order to present a proper historical context to the current problems of piracy, we cannot be bound by the current, very restrictive, UNCLOS definition of piracy. We are not alone in questioning the scope of UNCLOS's definition. Adam J. Young in his book, *Contemporary Maritime Piracy in Southeast Asia* defined piracy as:

> An act of boarding or attempting to board any ship with the intent to commit theft or any other crime and with the intent or capability to use force in the furtherance of that act, excepting those crimes that are shown or strongly suspected to be politically motivated.[27]

This definition eliminates both the two ship and the high seas limitations in UNCLOS but retains, albeit in the negative sense, the focus on private ends. The "capability of using force" appears broader than UNCLOS, as is the inclusion of "any other crime," whether violent or not. Cheating at cards on a gambling boat, or drinking underage as a passenger on a cruise ship, by someone with the "capability to use force," might satisfy Young's definition, but ought not constitute piracy. The International Maritime Bureau (IMB) essentially uses this definition, minus the final clause, in its reporting of piracy. The International Maritime Organization (IMO) defines any unlawful act of violence or detention or any act of depredation at anchor, off ports or when underway through a coastal state's territorial waters as armed robbery against ships.

A more appealing definition is also one of the earliest definitions of piracy. As mentioned earlier, Plutarch broadly defined pirates as those who attack without legal authority not only ships, but also maritime cities.[28] While this definition skirts the question of who can give legal authority, an important historical question, it seems to contain the roots of UNCLOS's exemption of attacks done under the authority of recognized states as piracy. It is broader in that the ship does not need to be on the high seas, and it includes, like current US law, attacks from the seas on coastal cities, which has historically been a common and lucrative pirate tactic. This definition is historically more inclusive of what societies meant when they used the term piracy. Part of the relevant history of piracy is how the act of piracy came to be so narrowly defined in modern convention.

Modern piracy

Modern piracy (like piracy in earlier ages) requires certain conditions to emerge and thrive. Pirates require a relatively safe haven on land, access to sea (particularly high-volume trade routes), and a weak or corruptible government. In this section we examine modern piracy, where it occurs and how it manifests itself around the globe using various business models. It is hard to talk about maritime piracy without falling into the Somali trap—that piracy is primarily a problem around Somalia. The authors of this book are guilty of perpetuating this myth as well. The fact is that piracy is a persistent global problem as shown in Figure 1.1. Although it dominates news headlines, Somali piracy is only a portion of the piracy events that have taken place over the last few decades.

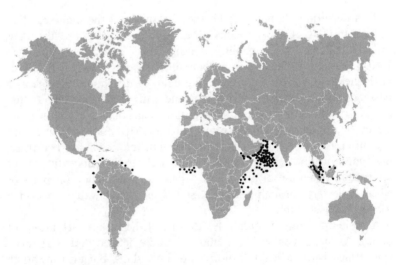

Figure 1.1 Locations of pirate attacks, 2010
Source: Data drawn from the IMB.

Although piracy occurs throughout the world, there are three main piracy hot-spots: the Malacca Strait, a narrow passage bordered by Malaysia, Singapore, and Indonesia; the Gulf of Guinea off the coast of Nigeria; and an increasingly large area off the coast of Somalia extending far out into the Indian Ocean. Before we describe piracy in each of these areas we offer a general explanation of three modern business models for piracy: kidnap and ransom, stealing the vessel and/ or its cargo, and robbing valuables from vessels in short raids. By far the most common piracy practice throughout the ages has been kidnapping. Crew, coastal residents and passengers were taken and then ransomed back to their countryman or sold into slavery. From Rome to Barbary to Somalia and Nigeria, people have been the most valued prize for most pirates.

What makes hostage taking appealing is that it does not depend upon port facilities. In some regions these facilities are inadequate for unloading the cargo of all but the smallest commercial vessels. The Somali hostage-taking model requires relatively secure off-shore sites where pirates can hold the ship until they complete the ransom. In places where retaining the ship is not feasible, such as Nigeria, hostages are taken off the ship and hidden on shore. According to Martin Murphy, Somali piracy is unique in that it is the only modern example of piracy in which pirates can hold vessels in their territorial waters indefinitely.[29]

Rather than taking hostages, pirates operating out of ports run by corrupt officials often steal cargo from the ship to resell on land. After unloading the cargo, pirates either sell the ship as scrap or re-register it under forged documents. Once the ship is re-registered they either use it for continuing criminal activity or sell it. This model of piracy is used in relatively small-scale piracy around Bangladesh where pirates capture fishing boats and their cargo of fish, forcing the crew overboard.[30]

In this model the hostages, rather than being the primary asset, become a liability and pirates have sometimes disposed of them *en masse*, as they did in the 1998 seizure of the *Cheung Song* when pirates killed the entire crew of 23 and threw their bodies overboard. They reason that the value of the cargo may be several times what pirates could recover through ransoms. Pirates may be able to negotiate a ransom of $10 million for the crew of an oil tanker but the oil is worth as much as ten times that amount. If the pirates can find a way to exploit the value of the oil, the profit derived from hijacking commercial vessels is greatly increased.

A third business model, which entails the robbery of ships' stores, equipment, cash, valuables, and the personal effects of crew members, is a low-grade form of piracy practiced throughout the world. This type of piracy is normally accomplished with a brief raid on a ship at anchor or underway. It occurs in areas where there is some criminal enforcement, but where black markets and fencing operations are prevalent. These are areas where it might not be safe to hold hostages and not possible to retain control of ships. This type of activity is prevalent around Bangladesh, the South China Sea, the Malacca Strait, Nigeria and in South America. While the economic gains are smaller, the violence can be intense. Pirates often assault (and sometimes kill) crew members in such raids. They have even abandoned vessels after a raid leaving no one in control of the moving ship. In the late 1970s and early 1980s this type of piracy was common in the Gulf of Thailand. The victims were the ethnic Han Chinese fleeing Vietnam in over-crowded refugee boats, many with their life's savings. Pirates abducted, raped and killed thousands of people in tens of thousands of pirate attacks over the decade. The governments in the area were not necessarily weak, but rather indifferent to the plight of the refugees.

These three business models are often, but not always, associated with a specific region. The three regions considered piracy hot-spots in 2011 are, as mentioned, Somalia, Southeast Asia, and Nigeria. The region receiving the most attention at that time was off the coast of Somalia, with pirates primarily being Somalis. Somalis attribute the emergence of piracy off their shorelines to two occurrences: the dumping of toxic waste on their coast and overfishing by foreign trawlers in the aftermath of the collapse of Somalia's government in 1991. In their narrative, piracy was a set of defensive actions undertaken by fishermen against illegal foreign fishing trawlers that took advantage of the governance gap in the aftermath of the collapse of the Somali government. International organizations including the United Nations have substantiated their claims that such incursions occurred. Since 1991 foreign fisherman poached between "$90 million and $300 million per year" from Somali waters.[31] Yet, regardless of any coast-guarding activity, from the beginning Somali pirates sought out and engaged merchant ships that had no relationship with illegal fishing or dumping.[32] By 2006, as pirate attacks moved far outside of Somali waters and ransom demands soared, any argument that Somali pirates were simply defending their coast was almost impossible to support. Figure 1.2 shows how pirate ventures started off the coast of Somalia in 2005 and moved as far east as the Maldives by 2011.

They have been able to extend their reach through the use of mother ships, or hijacked vessels that pirates use to attack other ships. Mother ships are larger, more durable vessels that allow pirates to travel farther from

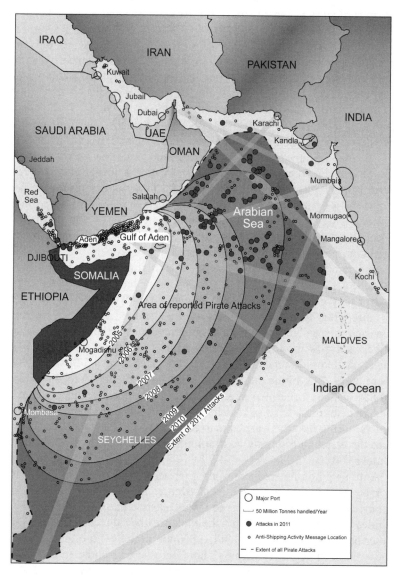

Figure 1.2 Threat map (2005–11)
Source: Geopolicity.

Somali shores. As a result of the extended region subject to pirate attacks, the area officially considered to be "high risk" was extended on 1 April 2011 to include all of the Arabian Sea and a larger portion of the Indian Ocean.[33]

As the Somali pirates' area of operations expanded so did the price they demanded in ransoms. In 2006 the average ransom was in the "hundreds of thousands of dollars" but by early 2011 the average payout was $5 million.[34] In April 2011 shippers paid an estimated 13 million to pirates to release the crude carrier *Irene SL*.[35] These activities corroborate our assertion that Somalis are not merely defending their coastline against foreign invaders. Poverty and access to the vital sea lanes connecting Europe and Asia may be more accurate drivers of Somali piracy. The $10,000 that a low-level pirate can earn from a ransom payment is significant in a country where the per capita gross domestic product (GDP) is $600 per year.[36] It is important to note, however, that while poverty may be a driver of piracy, it is the governance void that allowed its emergence. While Somali-based piracy targets mainly global shipping, pirates operating from the second piracy hotspot of Nigeria set their sights mainly on local targets. Because many of these attacks occur within Nigeria's territorial waters they are not piratical acts under international convention and go unreported to international monitoring centers. They are, however, reported internally although most observers believe that these statistics fall far short of reporting the actual numbers of attacks. Nevertheless, Nigeria's domestic reporting agency cites that between 2003 and 2008 there were 293 pirate attacks in Nigerian waters.[37] Violent pirate attacks against fishermen severely affected the local fishing industry. Nigerian journalists suggested in 2010 that 170 fishing trawlers were not venturing into the water due to fear of attack. They went on to say that the Nigerian economy was losing $600 million per year from these attacks.[38]

Although not as frequent, pirate attacks against global interests, namely the oil industry in the Niger Delta, can be dramatic. A typical attack would involve 2–3 speedboats carrying 20–30 pirates. The pirates are heavily armed and the violence they direct at the crew is described as "gratuitous."[39] Unlike Somali pirates, who often retreat if the crew members fire warning shots or otherwise indicate that they won't be taken without a fight, Nigerian pirates rarely back down. Similar to Somali piracy, the drivers of piracy in Nigeria are muddied between political grievances and personal greed on the part of the pirates. Nigerian pirates argue that they are defending Nigerians from the ecological and economic depredations of the government and multinational oil companies but most observers believe that greed plays the driving role. The third piracy hot-spot is Southeast Asia, where piracy has existed for thousands of years. Southeast Asia is the crossroad for trade between the Indian and Pacific oceans which currently connect Arabian Gulf oil to emerging economic powers of Asia.[40] Much of modern piracy occurs along the Malacca Strait, a narrow waterway bordered by Indonesia, Malaysia, and Singapore and the Singapore Strait. As of 2011, approximately 50,000 ships transit the Malacca Strait annually. It is 500 miles long and its narrowest navigable width is only a few miles wide, making it vulnerable to pirate attack. The Malacca Strait is integral to the global economy as approximately one-quarter of the world's seagoing cargo transit its waters.[41]

Southeast Asian piracy bears two distinct parallels to Nigerian piracy. First, many attacks are not piracy under international legal definitions because they occur within territorial waters. And second, although attacks on large commercial vessels command worldwide attention, the bulk of the attacks are aimed at fishermen and other local operators.[42] In 2005 for example 16 of the 18 reported attacks were against small, local vessels.[43] Attacks, however, run the gamut from simple robbery of ships in port to hijackings. Those conducting the attacks are "anyone from opportunistic fishermen, to members of syndicates, and even rogue military units."[44]

There was a marked decline in Southeast Asian piracy in the years 2004–6 but as of 2011 the number of incidents is rising again. No one is certain why piracy dipped in those years but there are a few competing hypotheses ranging from greater regional cooperation to the impact of the Tsunami in 2004. We discuss these in greater detail in Chapter 3.

Costs of piracy

There are continual attempts to trivialize piracy, from the entertainment industry's glamorization of pirates in books, movies, and Halloween costumes to the shipping companies who refuse to report attacks or minimize its impact on their business. But piracy is anything but trivial. It has been blamed for bringing down empires and it has catalyzed states to develop their navies. In the twenty-first century, piracy does not generally threaten states but its costs are nevertheless substantial. In the following section we briefly explore the current costs of piracy, disaggregating these costs into four categories—human, economic, environmental, and political.

Of these four costs the most significant is the cost in human welfare. In 2010 pirates hijacked 53 vessels and held 1,090 seafarers hostage.[45] Although data are not readily available on hostage welfare,[46] reports in the media suggest that as many as 21 of the 53 vessels hijacked in 2010 experienced "significant psychological or physical abuse, involving up to 488 seafarers."[47] Most notable were the execution of a hostage on the *Beluga Nomination* in retaliation for a failed rescue attempt in January 2011,[48] and the killing of four hostages aboard the US-flagged yacht, *SV Quest* in February 2011. The long-term psychological impact on the hostages is not yet documented, but the shipping community reports that many seafarers do not go back to sea after being held hostage.[49]

Somali pirates, in theory, do not intend to harm their hostages because their business model requires the safe return of hostages upon receipt of ransom payments. Until 2011 there was a perception that Somali pirates were generally abiding by this "gentlemen's agreement" not to harm hostages. But that year reports of torture and mistreatment began to publicly emerge. Table 1.1 shows the kinds of injuries that mariners sustained during pirate attacks, as outlined by the IMB. However, this does not document the abuse sustained during the period of captivity, the longer-term psychological trauma that many hostages experience or the violence against mariners committed in territorial waters.

Examples of reported torture include mock executions, beatings, and simulated drowning conducted over the side of the ship.[50] The knowledge that hostages were being tortured heightened the sense of urgency throughout the shipping community.

It is not only mariners who are hurt by piracy. Its impact is felt by coastal residents in regions where it flourishes. Somalis, for example, rely on food aid yet "piracy hinders the import and distribution of humanitarian aid to millions of Somalis on the verge of starvation."[51]

Table 1.1 Types of violence to crew (worldwide), 2006–10

	2006	2007	2008	2009	2010
Assaulted	2	29	7	4	6
Hostage	188	292	889	1,050	1,181
Injured	15	35	32	69	37
Kidnap/ransom	77	63	42	12	20
Killed	15	5	11	10	8
Missing	3	3	21	8	
Threatened	17	6	9	14	18
Total	**317**	**433**	**1,011**	**1,169**	**1,270**

Source: International Chamber of Commerce, *International Maritime Bureau.*

Pirates also steal or damage increasing numbers of local fishing vessels[52] negatively impacting the citizens of the Somali state of Puntland, both in their ability to earn an honest living and on their way of life. One fisherman from Eyl, once a pirate safe haven in Puntland, describes the risks that piracy presents for him and his community—"I no longer go fishing due to the increased number of foreign ships in the sea, it is too risky for us to go out there and fish. We fear that we may be mistaken as pirates and then get killed. ... It is not only the naval forces that we are afraid of but the pirates themselves; they sometimes take our boats by force to use them in hijacking. ... [Pirates] have introduced alcohol, massive inflation and commercial sex to the town, and that was not known to us before."[53] Many Somalis live in a state of fear due in part to piracy. A Somali woman from Eyl expressed her fears to a BBC reporter: " ... the pirates are too well-armed and now we hear reports that the West may launch airstrikes against us." Another local resident responded: "The people involved are outsiders. They've brought us nothing but trouble driving around day and night drinking and endangering our children."[54]

Yet while piracy has damaging effects on people its intended target is commerce. From the local fisherman to the global shipping company, pirates attempt to enrich themselves by taking what they want by force. Large shipping companies initially ignored piracy when it resurfaced as a major global issue or considered it someone else's problem.[55] In any year less than 1 percent of all ships are involved in a piracy event and 90 percent of those are relatively minor events, shippers felt that they could take their chances. In fact, it was not uncommon for ship owners to instruct their captains *not* to report incidences of pirate attacks. Shippers feared that an attack would raise their insurance premiums and that the legal prosecutions would tie up their ships and crews, costing them additional money.[56] They viewed pirate attacks and the subsequent ransom payment as simply a cost of doing business and they calculated that the cost of making all ships less vulnerable to attack outweighs the cost of the occasional pirate attack. Many of these costs do not fall on the maritime industry, and for an industry that has revenue of about $233 billion per year,[57] the industry's direct costs are modest. It is the upward trend that is troubling and shippers' calculations are evolving concurrently with these rising costs and increased risks to their crews. As mentioned previously ransoms paid to Somali pirates have skyrocketed. The total ransom payout for 2010 was approximately $238 million, not including excess costs associated with activities like negotiating ransoms and delivering the money.[58] The annual cost of piracy in 2010 is estimated to be between $7 billion and $12 billion, consisting mainly of the cost of re-routing ships to avoid piracy regions, naval operations in the Horn of Africa, prosecutions of pirate suspects, ransoms, and the steep rise in insurance premiums.

Ransoms are one form of direct economic costs of piracy, among many other direct and indirect costs. Direct costs include the cost of diverting ships around pirate-prone areas, increased insurance costs, increased crew costs, the cost of naval deployment, and the cost of prosecution. The indirect costs include effects on ancillary industries such as fishing, tourism, and oil, which reduce surrounding countries' gross domestic product, as well as reductions in overall global trade.

It has proven difficult to estimate accurately the indirect cost of piracy, especially because it is hard to separate the effects of piracy from the impact of general instability in piracy-prone regions. Anecdotal evidence from regional countries affected by piracy, does however, indicate indirect costs of piracy. The Seychelles reckons that piracy costs it around 4 percent of its GDP every year, mainly to its fishing and tourism industries.[59] The Kenyan Shippers Council estimates piracy increases the cost of imports by $23.8 million per month.[60]

These figures may underestimate the true cost that maritime piracy imposes on the global economy. For example, a significant mission of the Singapore Navy and the Singapore Police Coast Guard, which have a combined budget of almost $13 billion, is the suppression of piracy in the Singapore Strait, yet none of the costs of these organizations in Singapore have been included in calculations. Nor have the costs of similar organizations in China, the Philippines, Indonesia, Japan, nor in any other country been included in calculations for the cost of piracy. In part this is because they have successfully suppressed piracy in their immediate vicinity.

The economic costs of piracy accrue as well to individuals and states in the Horn of Africa. Livestock shipment, particularly cattle and goats, a significant business from Kenya to Mauritius was halted in 2009 because a suitable ship for the trade could not be found. The small ship that had been used was vulnerable to pirate attack. How much this will cost Kenyan ranchers and what it will do to the cost of beef in Mauritius has not been calculated although one annual contract was worth about $400,000—about 7 percent of Kenya's beef trade.[61]

Studies on the economic cost of piracy have received much media attention. The political costs of piracy, however, have been under-appreciated.[62] Piracy acts as a destabilizing effect on local politics in the regions where it flourishes, can foster corruption of government officials[63] and "can play a pivotal role in undermining and weakening government legitimacy" as was the case in Indonesia until about 2008.[64] In Somalia, New York Times reporter Jeffrey Gettleman reports that

Somali pirates are funding both sides of the civil war in that country.[65] Somali politicians benefit from the ransom money and further destabilize the region. The political costs relate to both the war lords' increases in power and the concomitant decrease in the influence of Somalia's official government, the Transition Federal Government (TFG).

Piracy in Nigeria has both local and national political costs. Locally, politicians may lose elections or gain support depending on their stances on oil companies—and militants. Nationally, piracy costs the government large sums of money each year. The Nigerian government receives approximately 80 percent of its revenue from oil, but pirates and rebels have cut off about 25 percent of the total it could be exporting.[66] Globally piracy costs governments untold sums of money in patrolling ships, trials, and antipiracy strategy. The opportunity cost of this is unknown, but surely, in an era of global recession money spent on piracy suppression could be put to other vital programs.

The fourth cost of piracy we discuss relates to its environmental impact. To date concerns over the environmental costs of piracy are largely hypothetical, and yet the potential for environmental devastation is alarming. Oil tankers are especially vulnerable to pirate attacks because they travel at relatively slow speeds, carry small crews, and have a low freeboard (height off the water). They are also vulnerable to catastrophic damage due to open fires or potentially explosive munitions fired at them. If a hijacked oil tanker is destroyed through mismanagement or intentional acts by pirates, an environmental disaster will ensue. A worrisome scenario is the destruction of a crude carrier in a place like Batu Berhanti, where the Strait of Malacca is only 1.5 miles wide. An attack here would cause massive environmental damage and could close one of the world's strategic transit points indefinitely.[67] In the 1978 Amoco Cadiz spill, a vessel very similar to the oil tankers that pirates are currently targeting and holding ran aground off the coast of France. The short-term effects of the spill included the death of millions of mollusks and sea urchins, birds and oysters, among other damaging effects. The damage caused in the semi-enclosed Gulf of Aden would be many times that experienced on the Atlantic coast of France, and the regional capacity to deal with such a spill is substantially less.

Conclusion

The purpose of this chapter was in part to dispel several misconceptions that surround piracy. Piracy is not an exotic event that occurred long ago, but rather an ongoing problem throughout modern history.

Contrary to conventional wisdom, piracy did not disappear from the seas after the Barbary pirates stopped plundering the Mediterranean. It has existed throughout the centuries and it is only the level of the modern-day threat that should surprise audiences.

Reading the newspaper in 2011 one might think that piracy is a crime committed only by young Somali men, and yet piracy occurs in many other parts of the seas as well. Maritime piracy is a global problem that manifests itself where pirates can find a relatively safe haven, access to sea, and a weak or corruptible government.

Throughout history, states have varied in their interpretation of what piracy was, and to what degree it could be legitimized by state approval. We carry this theme into Chapter 2 where we examine how this manipulation of definitions of piracy (and pirates themselves) encouraged and re-enforced piracy as a prominent feature in maritime history. Piracy is not a trivial problem. Its costs reverberate throughout societies in human, economic, political, and environmental realms. Understanding the nature of the problem is the first step in finding its solutions.

2 History

- **Ancient piracy**
- **Piracy after Rome**
- **Popular impressions of piracy**
- **Lessons for the twenty-first century**
- **Conclusions**

Terrible and glorious, villainous and romantic, anachronistic and modern, maritime piracy has had many faces throughout human history. In all of recorded history, maritime piracy has been one of the chronic perils of the seas and coastal people. From the Sumerian civilization of ancient Mesopotamia to the UN Security Council of today; from the Roman Republic to the empires of China, the powers of each era have attempted to deal with piracy either through military force, diplomacy, or they have ignored the problem altogether. At times, they have even encouraged it. Throughout history, piracy has been occasionally suppressed in one area, only to resurface later in the same area under more favorable conditions. The history of piracy raises the questions: why is it that sovereigns, empires, and states continue to have the same issues they have had throughout history? Can history assist us in developing strategies to suppress piracy?

In 2009, US Secretary of State Hillary Clinton, said "We may be dealing with a seventeenth-century crime, but we need to bring twenty-first century solutions to bear."[1] Acts of piracy have been a persistent feature of the last 40 centuries (including the eighteenth, nineteenth, and twentieth centuries). This chapter provides a brief review of the long history of sovereign, and later state interactions with piracy and provides policy advisors with an understanding of how specific suppression strategies came to be. It looks at some of the economic and political forces that led states to adopt specific views. It also addresses the paradoxical hold that pirates have had on the popular culture, and concludes with some of the lessons that can be drawn from history that are applicable to the suppression of modern piracy.

Ancient piracy

Around 2000 BCE, pirate attacks on the Sumerian civilization in Mesopotamia[2] were recorded in its cuneiform writings, one of the oldest written languages of humanity. Thucydides, writing in the late fifth century BCE, wrote that King Minos of Crete was the first sovereign to build a naval fleet to secure the sea from piracy. Until it was destroyed by a tsunami in 1400 BCE,[3] the fleet allowed Crete to colonize the Cycladic Islands, located between Greece and Crete, for nearly 300 years. Egyptian historians in the fourteenth century BCE recorded the Lukkans, a pirate people based on the southeast coast of Asia Minor, invading Cyprus and wiping away the remaining Minoan culture. By the thirteenth century BCE, the Lukkans had become a major disruption to Egypt. They had allied themselves to the Hittite Empire, which offered safe haven on land, in exchange for their naval power. A century later the Lukkans disappear from the historical record. It is likely that they were simply assimilated into a collection of maritime nomads and raiders known as the "sea peoples."[4] Around 1186 BCE, the Egyptians defeated the invading sea peoples. However, the remaining strength of the sea peoples was such that in 1160 BCE, the sea peoples toppled the Hittite empire, ransacked its capital Hattusas, and perhaps, precipitated the collapse of the Bronze Age cultures of the Eastern Mediterranean, ushering in a "dark age" in the ancient world lasting until 800 BCE.

In the ancient Mediterranean world, the concepts of "foreigner" and "enemy" were interchangeable, and piracy was a perfectly acceptable, even commendable, business practice as long as it was practiced against the people of a different tribe or nation.[5] Here the Greek historian Thucydides again discusses the occurrence of piracy before and during the ancient dark ages:

> For the Grecians in old time, and of the barbarians both those on the continent who lived near the sea, and all who inhabited islands, after they began to cross over more commonly to one another in ships, turned to piracy, under the conduct of their most powerful men, with a view both to their own gain, and to the maintenance for the needy, and falling upon towns that were unfortified, and inhabited like villages, they rifled them, and made most of their livelihood by this means; as this employment did not yet involve any disgrace, but rather brought with it somewhat of glory.[6]

The phrase "maintenance for the needy" and the statement that "their most powerful men ... made most of their livelihood by this means" suggest that these ancient people may have seen piracy as necessary for their survival. This same casual attitude is found in Homer's epics the *Iliad* and the *Odyssey.*

Maritime historian Henry Ormerod writes, "If we remember that piracy was, for centuries, a normal feature of Mediterranean life, it will be realized how great has been the influence which it exercised on the life of the ancient world."[7] The tremendous impact of piracy in that era is reflected in the geography of Europe today. Pirates historically attacked not only ships on the high seas but also engaged in extensive coastal raiding taking not only goods, but also lucrative hostages[8] who could be ransomed or sold as slaves. To protect against pirate attacks, great cities were built inland. For example, seventh century BCE Athens was built about seven miles inland from its port city of Piraeus.[9] Rome was founded nearly 20 miles from its port of Ostia during this same period.

European and ancient Southeast Asian cultures viewed piracy as "a way of accumulating power that eventually could be translated into legitimacy."[10] As an example, Queen Teuta of Illyria (Adriatic), who lived in the third century BCE, had ships that preyed upon the merchants of the Roman Republic. Authorizing her subjects' ships to prey[11] on her neighbors had already given her rank and power. She had no cause to question the successful state-building strategy. Queen Teuta had in the words of Alexander the Great's pirate captive 100 years earlier, been able to "take possession of cities, and subdue people." She was thus styled as a queen. The Roman Senate sent ambassadors to demand reparations and a cessation to the attacks. The queen told the ambassadors that according to Illyrian laws, piracy was lawful and that she had no business interfering with the advantages her subjects could get from the sea. One of the ambassadors replied that they would make it her business, which Rome did by defeating Queen Teuta in a two-year war.[12] While proclaimed by the Romans to be a pirate, and forced by defeat to surrender most of her lands to Rome's local allies, she is honored in her homeland for her resistance to Roman oppression. Her image appears on the reverse of the bimetallic, Albanian 100 leke coin issued in 2000.

Over much of the next 150 years, the chaos created by the expanding Roman Republic clashing with the already existing empires of Carthage in the West and the Macedonian and Seleucid Empires in the East allowed piracy to flourish. As pirate strength grew and Rome began to consolidate its power over the other empires, pirate targets increasingly became part of the Roman Empire. In 68 BCE, Ostia, Rome's own port, was sacked by Cilician pirates who also took two Roman senators as hostages. By this time, Cilician pirates were putting a stranglehold on Eastern Mediterranean trade, causing among other things, a grain shortage in Rome. According to Plutarch "the ships of the pirates numbered more than a thousand, and the cities captured by them four hundred. Besides, they attacked and plundered places of refuge and sanctuaries hitherto inviolate ..."[13]

The Roman senate responded to this blatant challenge to Roman supremacy by investing a decorated general, Gnaeus Pompeius Magnus (Pompey the Great), with the authority of a king. Pompey, taking advantage of his popularity among Roman citizens, pressured the senate to give him the resources to combat piracy, including "500 ships and 120,000 men."[14] Within three months Pompey's forces dramatically reduced piracy in the Roman Mediterranean. According to Pompey's report, his forces had destroyed at least 120 pirate bases, killed ten thousand pirates, mostly through battle, and destroyed 500 ships.[15]

There was no wholesale slaughter of captured pirates. Rather, Pompey's treatment of captured pirates was so humane that many pirates came to him with their families to surrender. These captured pirates helped Pompey's forces track down and punish those who had refused to surrender and were in hiding. According to Plutarch, Pompey reasoned "... that by nature man neither is nor becomes a wild or an unsocial creature, but is transformed by the unnatural practice of vice, whereas he may be softened by new customs and a change of place and life."[16] Pompey, unlike those before him, set about to help pirates find new pursuits that would not threaten Rome. He resettled them in fertile lands away from the coast where they could pursue non-threatening livelihoods. Except for the 20-year period of civil wars that followed Julius Caesar's crossing of the Rubicon in 49 BCE, levels of piracy in the Mediterranean remained low for four centuries until the collapse of the Western Roman Empire.

These ancient piracy events demonstrate three of the major ways that sovereigns or states can interact with pirates—collaboration, suppression, and tolerance. The Ancient Greeks, Queen Teuta, and the Hittites focused on collaboration believing it to be in their best interest. Queen Teuta's actions represent the beginning of what came to be called privateering. She authorized her subjects to prey upon Roman shipping and made piracy legal. The Hittites collaborated with pirates and used them to bolster their weak navy while Queen Teuta and the Greeks used pirates to build up territory and increase wealth.

The Greeks ultimately used their ill-gotten gains to consolidate their civilization. The second historical strategy was suppression and was used by King Minos, and later by Rome. In both cases, the use of military force and eventual occupation or disruption of the pirate's land-based communities was pivotal in suppressing piracy for centuries. The earlier Roman war against Queen Teuta had not been successful in ending piracy in the Adriatic Sea, but it was also not followed by annexation and occupation.

The third strategy—tolerance—was often the result of a state's distraction by other issues that posed more immediate threats. Such tolerance, or neglect, was a result of a simple cost-benefit analysis. Diverting resources to suppress piracy was not as important as existential threats. In Rome's case success in the last two Punic Wars and five Macedonian Wars was a more pressing concern. There also was a perceived value in trading with the pirates, further evidenced by Rome allowing pirate operations on the periphery of Roman lands. During these periods of neglect, ships and coastal towns had to depend on their own defenses. Many coastal communities became walled towns, and some, such as Piraeus, could close off their harbors with chains. As the acts of piracy became more acute, the cost of these defenses mounted, major ports were threatened, and economic disruptions became severe. Rome moved to suppression as its empire incorporated more Eastern provinces and brought Cilician territory into the center of the Roman economic world.

For many communities piracy was still viewed as a way of maintaining independence and wealth in an increasingly slave-dependent world marked by clashing empires. Pirate communities were parasitic communities taking the wealth of other, stronger powers, rather than producing their own wealth. Like other parasites that provide benefit to their hosts, piracy provided Eastern slaves to labor-short Italy and assisted in attacking Rome's enemies. Pirate communities, as parasites, thrived on the increasing wealth of Rome and on the decay and chaos caused by the rise and fall of major powers. Piracy thrived until Roman leaders recognized that the costs of piracy were falling more and more on its own economy and people, and moved to rid itself of the burden.

Piracy outside of the Mediterranean also shows a similar pattern. For example, the earliest official mention of piracy in China was in the Han Dynasty (206 BCE–220 CE) and "Thereafter, piracy tended to rise and fall with changes in regimes and the fluctuations of the economy. Whenever opportunities arose—during wars, natural disasters and economic depressions and the like—piracy occurred. It increased when governments were weak and either unable or unwilling to cope with the problem. It also increased when commerce was vibrant."[17] Natural disasters such as the tsunami that allowed the Lukkans to rise, encouraged piracy in China as well.

In the twenty centuries since this ancient period, sovereign and state responses to piracy remain collaborative, suppressive and tolerant, but ways of expressing these responses have changed dramatically. As discussed in Chapter 1, the evolution of international norms, laws, and political pressures have created significant change in the way modern states view piracy.

Piracy after Rome

The scourge of piracy continued even after Rome's success. From about 50 to 220 CE, piracy surged in China as the Han Dynasty came to an end. From the region of modern Denmark, Teutonic pirates— Angles, Saxons, and Jutes—raided coastal villages of Northern Europe and Britain, in the third century eventually settling the lands. These pirates were superseded by the Vikings in the ninth through twelfth century. Also common in the third and fourth centuries were the Gothic-Herulic pirates who operated in the Black Sea. In the fifth century, St. Patrick was kidnapped by Irish pirates.

Lacking official actions to suppress piracy around the Baltic and North Sea, the German merchants began in the twelfth century to form the Hanseatic League, a loose association for self-protection and regulation. By the middle of the next century the League began to dominate seaborne trade in Northern Europe. In 1259 the merchant associations (guilds) of Lübeck, Rostock, and Wismar declared:

> To all the faithful subjects of Christ ... Since most merchants are not protected on the sea from pirates and robbers, we have, in a common council, decreed, and by this writing declare, that all who rob merchants in churches, in cemetaries (sic), or on the water or on the land, shall be outlawed and proscribed by all cities and merchants. No matter where these robbers go with their booty, whatever city or land receives them shall be held equally guilty with them and proscribed by all the cities and merchants ...[18]

In 1265 the Decree of the Hanseatic League declared "If pirates appear on the sea, all the cities must contribute their share to the work of destroying them."[19] Even though these were declarations of merchant associations and not sovereigns, they continued the ancient tradition of holding the "cities or land" that provided safe havens to pirates "equally guilty" of the act of piracy. It is important to note that the cost of suppressing piracy was known to be high and was to be shared among all the merchants. During this time the League rivaled the power of territorial sovereigns, defeating the King of Denmark in war in 1370. After the start of the fourteenth century the League transformed. It became a network of agreements between the merchant cities themselves, and remained active for at least another 200 years until competition, the rise of the territorial state, and the development of global empires overpowered it in the seventeenth century.

The emerging global empires of Portugal and Spain reduced the importance of Baltic merchants starting with the voyages of discovery by Columbus in 1492 and Vasco da Gama in 1497. These voyages were themselves driven by the fall of Constantinople in 1452 and the rise of the Ottoman Empire inspired piracy in the Eastern Mediterranean which made the traditional trade routes to Asia unsafe.[20] Over the next 400 years the waxing and waning European and Asian Empires including the Spanish, Dutch, English, French, Ottoman, Chinese, Malay, Mogul, and others created a fertile ground for piracy to flourish.

The clashes between these warring empires resulted in three significant episodes of piracy. First, the growth of piracy based on the Barbary coast of North Africa which lasted until the French invasion of North Africa in the 1830s; second, the successful contesting of Spanish and Portuguese claims to foreign colonies and ocean trade by other European sovereigns that culminated in the end of the Golden Age of Piracy in 1726; and third, the high levels of Asian piracy in response to instability in Asia brought about by European incursions and their efforts to protect trade routes. This lasted well into the nineteenth century.

Piracy along the Barbary Coast had been going on for centuries, but the defeat of the Moors in Granada in 1492 drove many into exile. The pirates retaliated with raids on the European coasts, and after 1518 received aid from the Ottoman Empire until shortly after the battle of Lepanto in 1571. This significantly reduced the Ottomans' sea power and influence. Barbary piracy was massive. For example in 1544, the Island of Lipari, off the coast of Sicily, was attacked and nine thousand inhabitants were taken as slaves.[21] In all, from the sixteenth to the nineteenth century, up to one-and-a-quarter million Europeans were captured by Barbary pirates, mostly from coastal raids as far north as Iceland.[22]

Barbary piracy was able to last for centuries in part because the emerging powers of the day sought to use it to their advantage. "That such an iniquity was more or less tolerated for centuries is one of the curiosities of history. It can only be explained by the fact that European nations found it a convenient scourge for their enemies. France and England especially were continually intriguing to make infamous treaties with the Dey (of Algiers) to the benefit of each against the other."[23] The fact that various states paid tribute to the Barbary pirates meant that the flag flown by a merchant ship became an increasingly important element in its defense. Venetian merchants in the seventeenth and eighteenth centuries often used the English flag as a means of evading the Barbary Pirates. Since the English paid tribute, and were respected as a naval power able to inflict damage on the pirate communities, English ships were often allowed safe passage by the Barbary pirates. By flying the English flag, Venetian merchants freebooted on the English power.[24]

The flag of a ship has had importance from the ancient times. According to Polyaenus, in the fourth century BCE, Queen Artemisia of Halicarnassus, naval ally of Xerxes in the invasion of Greece, carried two different flags on her vessels. She would fly the Persian standard while chasing Greeks, but would fly a Greek standard when she was being chased.[25] This is perhaps the earliest record of "reflagging" a vessel for piratical activity or for defense. Over time the responsibility of a sovereign for the ships that sailed under their flag became more established. The sovereign was recognized as having responsibility for both the defense of ships flying their flag and for the actions of such ships. As J.K. Mansell writes "The flag has come to be an officially sanctioned and very powerful symbol of the state and is the visible evidence of the nationality conferred by the state upon ships registered under its national law."[26]

Historically, a ship sailing under the flag of a sovereign was representing itself as sailing under the authority and protection of that sovereign, to whom it often had close physical and political connections. When states acted to suppress pirates, it was often because the attacks on their national ships were direct attacks on their citizens and their economic interests. When President Thomas Jefferson sent the new US Navy to Tripoli in 1801 to fight the Barbary pirates, US-flagged ships carried roughly 90 percent of the new country's foreign commerce.[27] About 20 percent of America's exports were destined for Mediterranean ports where wheat and tobacco were exchanged for figs and carpets.[28] American independence meant that the tribute paid by England, and the English navy's power, no longer secured American-registered ships from piracy. The ship owners, sailors, merchants, and farmers of the new state had enough political power to ensure that the new government defended their interests. Even so, during the war of 1812 American ships often took the flag of Portugal to avoid English privateers.[29]

The laws of the state where ships were registered applied on the ships. Ships were considered the territory of their flag state, so that an attack on the ship was an attack on the state. States could not legally impose their laws on the ships of other states. Often ships of one flag were restricted from trading in ports of another flag or even sailing in the seas claimed by another state, laws typical of the mercantile philosophy prevalent at the time.

These restrictions on travel and trade on the high seas were the proximate cause of the second major episode of piracy after 1492. By the authority of the Pope Alexander VI, the Treaty of Tordesillas in 1494 and the Treaty of Zaragoza in 1529 divided the oceans of the world between Spain and Portugal.[30] Other European powers, primarily the Dutch, English, and French, contested this division. They fostered and encouraged piracy with letters of marque; legal documents which gave the merchant/privateer license to commit violence largely because their navies were inadequate to fight the power of the period. Unlike the Spanish, they could not station naval fleets in the Caribbean and Indian Oceans. It was asymmetrical warfare rather than direct engagement. The powerful Spanish and Portuguese fleets against the weaker states with their commissioned privateers. The Spanish and Portuguese were amassing vast fortunes of gold and silver from the New World and spice from the Indian Ocean region[31] and the ships that transported these riches were vulnerable to attack. In this case, a state's collusion with pirates was a critical way of weakening its enemies, exerting far greater force than their limited government revenues would support, and opening trade routes and colonial expansion to their people.

American colonists played their part in encouraging piracy during its "Golden Age," through their economic and security engagements with pirates. The reasons for collusion had to do with the English Navigation Acts. They "mandated that only ships built, owned and registered in Britain could trade with American colonies, that the master and three-quarters of the crew be British, and that merchandise freight going to or from any other European country to the American colonies must make a stop in England to pay a duty."[32] It also forbade colonists from trading with any other nations. Consequently the price of everyday items became exhorbitant. Pirates took full advantage of the colonists' ready market for the goods they had plundered.

Colonists relied upon the pirates, who brought relatively cheap goods from as far away as India and Madagascar, and in return, provided the pirates with relatively safe harbors to refit their ships. Many colonial governors were implicated in this collusion. William Markham, the governor of Pennsylvania from 1694 to 1699, echoing statements by Queen Teuta two thousand years earlier, said that "if the seamen brought good solid income to Philadelphia, it wasn't his affair to ask how they got it."[33] Indeed, when these pirates were captured, Governor Markham posted their bail and had them released. The Pennsylvania Governor obviously did not frown on the culture of the pirate as one pirate eventually married his daughter.[34]

The end of the Golden Age of Piracy began at the turn of the eighteenth century. The English navy had become so dominant that they no longer needed privateers to serve as an auxiliary force.[35] When the War of Spanish Succession ended, the English and their American colonists began a campaign to demonize pirates. Peace treaties between the European powers resulted in the nullification of the privateers' commissions. No longer legally sanctioned by states, many privateers turned to pure piracy, augmented by thousands of former navy sailors and officers who were discharged after the war.

At the same time, territorial boundaries in the Americas had been largely established. Agriculture, with its demand for slave labor, had taken over as the main source of wealth and the colonial economies came to rely on stability and enslaved Africans to prosper. The pirates started causing massive disruption to slavers including the predation of hundreds of slave ships. According to pirate historian, Markus Rediker, "Pirates had ruptured the Middle Passage, and this would not be tolerated."[36,37] Political pressure against piracy became more vocal. The 1698 English law for the more effective suppression of piracy set up Vice-Admiralty courts, which allowed pirates to be tried outside of England.[38] Colonial officials aided this effort by enacting severe penalties, including death for any colonist who aided the pirates, thereby instilling tremendous fear in the colonial populations.

At one of the many public executions of pirates in the American colonies, minister Cotton Mathers exclaimed, "All nations agree to treat your Tribe as *the Common Enemies of Mankind*, and [to] extirpate them out of this world."[39] Another minister cried, "fearfulness and horror should overwhelm him; a dreadful sound should be in his ears of the Destroyer coming on him; Trouble and anguish shall make him afraid."[40] Between 1716 and 1726, 400–600 men were executed under this court system.[41] These executions were part of a brutal public relations campaign aimed at terrorizing all who had witnessed them, or who would read about their lurid details. If the executions were not forceful enough, British and American bailiffs provided grim reminders by sometimes placing a pirate's corpse on public view until his flesh rotted away—a process that sometimes took as long as two years. Executions were not the only way that the British suppressed piracy. They also offered general amnesties to pirates, including the general amnesty offered by King George I in 1717 to all those who gave up piracy before September of 1718.

The third great outbreak of piracy occurred in Asia, partially homegrown and partially fueled by the chaotic arrival of the Europeans. The Ming Dynasty's harsh controls over trade and sea routes had the effect of sending coastal residents into the arms of pirates. During the 1500s, emperors banned trade between their subjects and overseas merchants, from both Japan and Europe. They required their subjects to get permission before they set sail for foreign territory, and even at times banned fisherman from fishing. The combination of these harsh measures both contributed to, and coincided with, a series of devastating famines starting in 1538 that limited the government's ability to feed the people. This brought about an explosion in piracy.

The pirates of China from roughly 1520 to 1870 became an empire onto themselves. At their height they were approximately 70,000 strong.[42] They operated thriving black markets throughout China that brought livelihood to villagers that had largely been overlooked, providing goods at prices much cheaper than those available through more licit means.[43] Although the locals started colluding with the pirates, state-sponsored privateering was not a common practice in Asia until it was introduced by Europe, most notably through the activities of the Dutch East India Company. The Dutch East India Company, in the seventeenth century was the most highly capitalized public company in the world and operated out of Batavia (modern day Jakarta) under a Dutch royal charter that gave it the right to conduct war and foreign policy in its own name. It established a colonial base in Southwest Taiwan in 1624 and when the Chinese refused to grant them free trade the company ventured into privateering, paying Chinese pirates to attack Chinese merchants and bring a larger quantity of better priced merchandise to the Dutch merchants.

The Qing Dynasty, which ousted the Ming Dynasty in 1644, enacted severe measures to quell piracy. They mandated that coastal people burn their boats and banned the construction or purchase of large junks. They instituted a policy of capital punishment for any merchant who went out to sea. Remarkably, they even forced coastal villages to relocate 20 miles inland in order to deny pirates functioning ports or potential targets. Still, unable to suppress the pirates on their own, Chinese authorities also enlisted the help of Europeans who had come to East Asia in search of trading partners. The most effective Chinese tactic was to offer full pardons to pirates. Many pirate leaders accepted these pardons and even turned pirate hunter. In 1810 Chinese pirate, Cheung Po Tsai (Zheng Bo) became a venerated imperial admiral.[44] The remaining pirate fleets were demoralized and much easier for the Chinese and Europeans to break. By the late-nineteenth century they largely succeeded in clearing the South China Sea of large-scale pirate activity.

Popular impressions of piracy

It is important to draw a distinction between the way that states have defined pirates (as discussed in Chapter 1, as criminals, combatants, or allies) and the way that pirates have been perceived by the general population of their nations and of their victims. Pirates have long been objects of fascination and the history of piracy is replete with Barbarians who became nobles and lowly maritime predators who became folk heroes. This perception is an intriguing part of the history of pirates, and its roots are much longer than might be expected by those who believe that the public fascination with pirates started with *Treasure Island* or Long John Silver.

As discussed previously, Queen Teuta is still honored in Albania for her resistance to Roman rule. In China, nineteenth-century pirate Zheng Chenggong (or Koxinga), who even before his death had become a Chinese folk hero, was actually deified upon his death. There are several large temples and monuments dedicated to him in Xiamen and Taiwan where he remains a hero of several competing political groups.[45] Sir Francis Drake and Sir Henry Morgan were only two of many pirates knighted by their countries. To the British, American "naval hero" John Paul Jones was a pirate, and the Barbary pirates claimed to be part of an Islamic jihad against Christian crusaders. Jean Lafitte was undoubtedly a pirate in 1814 in Louisiana but in return for a pardon for himself and his men, he helped Andrew Jackson defeat the British attack on New Orleans in 1815. His men were praised for the accuracy of their gunnery which had a devastating impact on the British forces.[46]

In more modern times, authors such as Robert Louis Stevenson and Howard Pyle drew vivid images of pirates as free-spirited adventurers. Piracy was such a fascination that in 1908 one of the first motion pictures made was a short, *The Pirates Gold.* Since then more than 300 pirate movies have been made including two of the top-ten highest grossing movies of all time in Disney's *Pirates of the Caribbean* series,[47] which casts the life of a pirate as a roguish adventurer flummoxing the hidebound and dull-witted authorities. A favorable public viewpoint extends to modern piracy. Somali pirates present a narrative that casts them as the defenders of their homeland, in much the same model that Queen Teuta adopted.[48] This viewpoint is repeated by groups sympathetic to the pirates' claims that they are protecting Somalia's fish stocks from poaching and their seas from the dumping of toxic waste. Indeed the Transitional Federal Government (TFG) legislature was unable to pass an anti-piracy law in January 2011 because too many of the legislators saw them in this heroic light.[49] The historical fascination with piracy has ancient roots, and in part helps to explain why some societies give space for pirates to operate.

Lessons for the twenty-first century

This historical overview represents a brief introduction to the way that states have interacted with pirates throughout history and provides a number of lessons. Along with Chapter 1, this history shows that views of and interactions with pirates have evolved as the international context and economic and political pressures have changed. Throughout this history, there are several themes which reoccur and which are important to extract. These themes include the central role of economic issues, the development of piracy in criminal law, and the role that flag states and coastal states have played in the development and suppression of piracy.

Pirates are primarily motivated by economic gain, even when the act has some political benefits for others. Unchecked, or encouraged, piracy can have an enormous impact on legitimate trade and even state power. Piracy largely prevented Spain and Portugal from building dominant empires, and allowed England, France, and The Netherlands to contest and weaken much stronger powers. The impact of piracy, as privateering, fell mostly on the merchants. Alfred Rubin, a scholar of piracy law, notes that laws on piracy were written to safeguard "private property crossing national boundaries."[50]

It is not coincidental that piracy began to be criminalized when private property and trade began to become important for a state's economic success. By the end of the seventeenth century the business leaders in some European countries began to rival the landed nobility in wealth and property. In England in particular the younger children of noble families' would go into business and with wealth and connection they were able to influence state policies. While the first English law to criminalize piracy, the Offences at Sea Act, passed in 1536, it was only in 1698 that parliament created colonial piracy courts. Privateering continued to be so disruptive, and privateers so hard to control, that the Declaration of Paris in 1856 outlawed piracy. For the first time it internationalized piracy as a criminal activity within an international system. The significance, and success of this, will be discussed in greater detail in later chapters.

The history also shows that the country where a ship was registered and whose flag it flew became increasingly important. Ships were protected and regulated by the laws and military forces of their flag state. A good example is that in the middle of the nineteenth century the problem of piracy was so severe around Hong Kong that the British began registering Chinese ships in Hong Kong, and authorized them to fly the British flag as part of an anti-piracy convoy policy. But in 1856, local Chinese authorities who considered all Chinese owned ships to be their responsibility, boarded the Hong Kong registered *Arrow*, lowered the British flag, and arrested 12 Chinese crew members. Local British officials claimed the act was an insult to the British flag and the British went to war. On 1 May 1857, the British Navy engaged and defeated a Chinese fleet.

As piracy declined as an issue, particularly after the Declaration of Paris and into the twentieth century, flying the flag of a military power was seen as less beneficial. The naval powers were drawing up costly plans to mandate stronger hulls in their merchant ships so they could be armed and serve as a naval auxiliary in time of war.[51] When war broke out, it was risky to fly the flag of a belligerent state. At the beginning of the First World War, the British government even encouraged their ships to fly the neutral American flag, an act for which the United States formally complained. Also, social legislation in the more developed countries were increasing costs or affecting ship operations. At the suggestion of the US Shipping Board, two US-owned cruise ships were the first to seek registry in Panama so they could serve alcoholic drinks during prohibition.[52]

As the Second World War approached, ships re-registered under a neutral flag in countries that permitted "open registry," or the registry of ships without any meaningful connection between the owner and the state. The first to officially offer such a registry was Panama in 1925. The neutral flag offered *de jure*, but often not *de facto*, protection from the belligerents. Neutral states were not only a bit safer, but also made fewer fiscal and technical demands on owners. Owners were quick to see the economic advantages of open registries after the conflicts were over. Despite the carnage of war, Panama's fleet doubled in size between the start of war and 1947.[53] The attitudes of owners had changed considerably. Greek ship owner Stavros Niarchos wrote in 1950 that "A ship owned by a national from a particular country loads in a second one, unloads in a third country and finally trades with a fourth. I must confess I do not believe in any valid reason to justify that this ship must have one flag rather than another. Maritime trade has always been, and must carry on being, an international business."[54] The economic incentives drove many more shippers to the open registry. The result is that today more than 55 percent of the global fleet is registered in the open registry states.[55] The shift in the capabilities of the flags under which the majority of ships sail is a major change in the history of merchant shipping, and a significant contributor to the development of modern piracy as will be discussed in Chapter 5.

In all the instances discussed, it is clear that piracy requires onshore support to thrive, and often has required on-shore action to resolve. Control of coastal ports has always been the most effective and first line of defense against piracy. When ports could not or would not stop piracy, dominant powers would destroy, occupy, or colonize these ports—acts that would not be sanctioned by twenty-first century international norms. Indeed, much of the European colonial expansion was driven by the need to protect trade from pirate attacks. In the case of modern piracy, this suggests that coastal states are key actors in the resolution of problems of piracy, but, as discussed in Chapter 1, this does not yield an easy solution. The modern locations where piracy thrives are areas where the capacities of the coastal states are seriously diminished and international intervention is both costly and limited.

Conclusion

When the first line of defense against piracy—the coastal state, fails and piracy develops into a more systematic problem, the nations whose ships are preyed upon, the flag states, historically have become the second line of defense. The aggressive Roman, Chinese, and British campaigns against pirates were driven by the impact that the pirates' depredations were having on their own ships and economies. With open registries, the second line of defense has been severely undermined. The Hanseatic League represented a third line of defense when neither the coastal states nor the flag states would protect shipping: the merchant societies and shipper took responsibility for their own defense. This was also used by the various West and East Indian companies during the expansion of European empires. In all these instances these organizations developed military power that could threaten territorial sovereigns and they were eventually taken over by sovereigns or liquidated.

Modern piracy suggests that modern international systems have not adequately adjusted to the diminished capacity of flag states to intervene, nor developed an alternative to military intervention and occupation when piracy is not controlled by a coastal state. The industry has only recently begun to look at various self-protection schemes, and the implications of such a private projection of military power have not been well-examined.

In the next chapter we look at both public and private international institutions and organizations that have been developed over the last century to ensure maritime security. In particular we examine what capacity these institutions actually have to address modern piracy.

3 The nuts and bolts of twenty-first century maritime governance relevant to combating piracy[1]

- Global intergovernmental organizations
- Regional intergovernmental organizations
- International military response
- Non-governmental organizations

States acknowledge that tackling piracy requires international cooperation. As such, there is no shortage of regional and international organizations that are devoted to combating piracy. These bodies represent some of the first modern attempts to form transnational governance systems to deal with piracy. But although the global response to piracy is impressive in terms of the level of effort undertaken by these organizations, the results are not. Piracy persists and is worsening, leaving many to question why this complex system isn't significantly reducing its incidence. We submit that there are three main problems with the international effort: there is more competition between institutions than cooperation; there is overlap among the institutions; and the efforts are not focused on goals or metrics for measuring success—simple cooperation seems to be the end-goal. Figure 3.1 illustrates the point that a multitude of organizations are working with the same mandates and this overlap may hinder a successful response to piracy. In this chapter we look at the most prominent of these global and regional efforts to combat piracy.

Global intergovernmental organizations

The United Nations (UN) plays a leading role in countering piracy on a global scale. The UN system is "designed to organize international cooperation in a coherent fashion by bringing the United Nations, invested with the power of scope, into relationship with various autonomous and complementary organizations, invested with sectoral

Initiative	Operations		Capacity Building		Self-Protection
	Maritime Ops	Info Sharing	Rule of Law	Operational	
Contact Group on Piracy off the Coast of Somalia (CGPCS)	X	X	X	X	X
Djibouti Code of Conduct				X	X
ESA-IO Reional Strategy and Regional Plan of Action				X	X
EU	X				X
International Maritime Bureau Piract Reporting Centre (IMB PRC)		X			
International Maritime Organization (IMO)			X		
INTERPOL			X		
Kampala Process	X				
League of Arab States				X	
Malacca Strait Patrols	X	X			
Maritime Organization of West and Central Africa (MOWCA)	X		X	X	X
NATO	X				X
New York Declaration					X
Out of Area Nations	X	X		X	
Port and Coastal Nations	X	X		X	X
Regional Agreement on Countering Piracy and Armed Robbery against Ships in Asia (ReCAAP)		X			X
Shared Awareness and Deconfliction (SHADE)		X			
The African Union				X	
UKMTO		X			X
United Nations Security Council, General Assembly and Secretary General	X		X	X	X
United Nations Development Programme (UNDP)					
United Nations Office on Drugs and Crime (UNODC)		X	X	X	
U.S. and Combined Maritime Forces (CMF)	X			X	X
World Maritime Day 2011 - "Piracy: Orchestrating the Response"				X	

Figure 3.1 Multinational initiatives
Source: Oceans Beyond Priacy.

powers."[2] In this section we discuss the many ways that the UN is working with other global institutions to counter piracy.

After the establishment of the UN in 1945, its member states decided to create an institution that would safeguard life at sea. Previously shipping had been a "highly individualized industry, extremely competitive both nationally and internationally and in the western world interference by governments was looked upon askance."[3] To remedy this situation, the UN created the Inter-Governmental Maritime Consultative Organization (now the IMO), which subsumed several *ad hoc* conventions under its umbrella. The IMO operates a specialized agency in the UN system, overseeing UN activities relevant to the safety, security, and environmental impact of ships. It has adopted several international conventions relevant to piracy for its member countries to implement. These conventions include the Convention for the Suppression of Unlawful Acts Against the Safety of Maritime Navigation (SUA), the Safety of Life at Sea Convention (SOLAS), the International Convention on Standards of Training, Certification and Watchkeeping for Seafarers, and the International Ship and Port Facility Security Code (ISPS Code).[4]

The IMO promotes regional cooperation as the key to bringing down levels of piracy. To that end it brought together 17 Middle Eastern and African states in the Somali region that adopted the Djibouti Code of Conduct concerning the Repression of Piracy and Armed Robbery against Ships in the Region (Djibouti Code) in January 2009, discussed later in the chapter. The IMO also assists countries with maritime security-related capacity-building through the Integrated Technical Cooperation Programme, a train-the-trainers program that addresses maritime security issues. It also serves as a tracking center for data about the ships that are attacked including the location of an attack and information about how the crew and other groups responded to the attack and were affected by the attack.[5]

The IMO is not the only UN-sponsored organization working on piracy issues. The UN Security Council (Security Council) has addressed maritime piracy and armed robbery in the Somali context in resolutions 1976, 1816, 1846, 1851, 1897, 1918, and 1950. The UN General Assembly (General Assembly) has addressed piracy in resolution 64/71. Table 3.1 describes these resolutions.

As requested by Security Council resolution 1918, the UN Secretary-General outlined seven options for prosecuting and imprisoning pirates.[6] In January 2011, a newly appointed special advisor on piracy, Jack Lang, presented to the Security Council an additional 25 proposals to combat piracy.[7]

Table 3.1 UN General Assembly and Security Council resolutions

Resolution	Substance	Date
1816 (Security Council)	Allows states to enter territorial waters of Somalia for a period of six months to repress acts of piracy (with consent of the TFG)	2 June 2008
1846 (Security Council)	Urged state parties to the SUA convention to fully implement their obligations to build judicial capacity	2 December 2008
1851 (Security Council)	Allows states to conduct land-based missions in Somalia for a period of 12 months with support of the TFG	16 December 2008
1897 (Security Council)	Urges states to strengthen capacity in Somalia to stop piracy. Extends 1816 for successive one-year periods	30 November 2009
1950 (Security Council)	Extends 1851 for successive one-year periods	23 November 2010
1976 (Security Council)	Condemns the practice of hostage-taking noting the severe impact it has on both the hostages and their families	11 April 2011
64/71 (General Assembly)	Calls upon states to take appropriate steps under their national law to apprehend and prosecute suspected pirates. Urges states to adopt national anti-piracy legislation	4 December 2009
1918 (Security Council)	Requests that the secretary-general present a report (within three months) on options for prosecuting and imprisoning pirates operating off the coast of Somalia	27 April 2010

Source: United Nations.

The Security Council resolutions have provided moral support to countries willing to become involved with counterpiracy, but their substantive impact has been much smaller. For example resolutions 1816 and 1897 allow foreign warships to enter Somalia's territorial waters, but only with the approval of the Transitional Federal Government (TFG). The resolutions create no new legal authorities as states can always give authority for foreign warships to operate in their territorial waters. The Security Council also made it explicit that this action applied only to Somalia and could not be construed as a precedent setting for territorial waters in other piracy prone regions. These provisions primarily served to recognize the UN-established TFG as the national government of Somalia.

Although the resolutions offer valuable advice to states in addressing piracy, they are non-binding. They can urge states to act but they cannot force them to do so. For instance, the General Assembly in resolution 64/71 called for countries to implement national codes to criminalize piracy and yet many states have not done so. Some states have criminalized piracy but their codes are outdated. In most cases states that have not criminalized piracy cannot prosecute suspected pirates. They must turn a captured pirate over to another state that is willing or able to prosecute or they must release the alleged pirate. Many states as well are not willing to prosecute pirates unless they have a direct connection to an attack, that is, a ship flying their flag was attacked or their nationals injured.

Another attempt to respond to Somali piracy was the creation of the Contact Group on Piracy off the Coast of Somalia (Contact Group) in 2009. Its aim is to facilitate discussion and coordination of action among states and organizations fighting piracy and armed robbery at sea. Any state or international organization making a tangible contribution to the counterpiracy effort, or any country significantly affected by piracy off the coast of Somalia may become a member of the Contact Group. Other relevant stakeholders may participate in the meetings of the Contact Group and its four Working Groups as observers. Until the seventh plenary session in November 2010, the Contact Group met on an ad hoc basis. However, members decided to meet on a regular basis three times per year, in March, July, and November. Decisions must be taken by consensus by the members of the Contact Group.[8]

The Contact Group has links to the UN but is not officially under their aegis. It views piracy as "one element of a larger challenge"— namely the reintroduction of political and economic stability within Somalia. Clearly spelling this out in the final communiqué of the 6th plenary session, they write, "Participants in the Contact Group also agree that a viable solution for piracy will not be achieved unless peace and stability in Somalia are restored."[9] The Contact Group provides a forum for exchange of information and ideas, and coordinates the efforts of states and relevant organizations through four working groups discussed below.

Working Group 1 promotes military and operational coordination between the navies involved in counterpiracy operations off the coast of Somalia with particular focus on the Gulf of Aden, the Internationally Recognized Transit Corridor (IRTC), and in the Somali Basin. Members of Working Group 1 have agreed on a number of concrete steps to mitigate threats such as extending the use of industry Best Management Practices or BMP (BMP defines a set of recommendations on how ships may be operated to prevent and defend against pirate attacks), increasing the use of military Vessel Protection Detachments for vulnerable shipping, increasing the number of military assets available for the operations, and possibly increasing land-basing options in the region to support the ongoing counterpiracy operations.

In 2009 Working Group 1 carried out a regional counterpiracy capability development needs assessment and prioritization mission to East Africa and the Gulf of Aden. The mission report was endorsed by the Contact Group in January 2010 as the basis for future work to address counterpiracy capability needs in the region. The needs assessment report recommended that: implementation of the Djibouti Code should underpin all regional counterpiracy activity; any activity, particularly in Somalia, should support the political process; solutions should be comprehensive and include penal/judicial legislation, prosecution, media and communications, community involvement, and alternative livelihoods as well as kinetic (military-based) counterpiracy capabilities; and national/sub-national training requirements should be matched with regional and international training opportunities.[10]

Working Group 2 addresses legal issues related to piracy. Discussions in this working group have addressed issues such as the use of force in a maritime law enforcement context, the application of human rights obligations to the apprehension, detention and the transfer of suspects, impediments to national prosecutions, and the needs of regional states for capacity-building. Several possible judicial mechanisms being considered are described in the UN secretary-general's report of July 2010 on possible options to further the aim of prosecuting suspects of piracy and/or armed robbery at sea.

Working Group 3 addresses ways to strengthen shippers' self-defense against pirate attacks. It works closely with the IMO, the shipping industry, and other industry groups to promote counter-piracy measures such as the BMP and ISPS Codes. Working Group 4 is a public relations campaign intended to convince Somalis that piracy is wrong. Their main project, "utilizing media to prevent and combat piracy in Puntland," has been criticized as to its utility and importance when compared with other projects. In response, the working group has been tasked with charting their progress in a "yearly progress questionnaire." Because little information is available on this working group, the public perception is that very little work has been done.

The Contact Group has been criticized for being both too open and too closed. Some say that it is too state-centric and not open to non-governmental stakeholders. Conversely it is criticized for being too inclusive—the large number of attendees at the working groups hinders dialogue, strategy coordination, and concrete action.

While the Contact Group can make recommendations it must rely on agencies within the system to implement these recommendations. One such agency is the UN Office on Drugs and Crime (UNODC), which launched a counterpiracy program in 2009 to enhance criminal justice capacity among Somalia's neighbors. Its mandate is to ensure that the trial and imprisonment of suspected pirates is humane, efficient, and takes place within a sound rule-of-law framework. The UNODC has worked with Kenya, Mauritius, the Seychelles, and Tanzania to review the national legal codes and make sure they are consistent with international laws and human rights norms. This has also included training workers in the legal system and improving court facilities. The project has introduced best management practices for investigation to the police in Kenya and the Seychelles.[11] The UNODC is also investing in the restoration of the rule of law in Somalia.[12]

While the UNODC addresses judicial challenges, the UN Development Programme (UNDP) has focused on governance, security, and economic development systems. This has included an explicit focus on piracy through programs aimed at supporting judicial programs in Somaliland and Puntland. Additional programs have included legal aid programs for suspected pirates as well as support for new prisons and police training.[13] The UNDP also supports literacy programs for prisoners in Puntland.[14]

The UN also recognizes that non-UN organizations can play a vital role in counterpiracy. The International Criminal Police Organization (INTERPOL) is one of these organizations. INTERPOL facilitates international cooperation between police forces to prevent international crime.[15] The Security Council recognized the importance of INTERPOL in the fight against piracy in two separate resolutions "urging all member countries to cooperate with INTERPOL to secure successful prosecutions."[16] The resolution specifically implored states to make sure piracy is criminalized under their domestic laws, to focus on financial flows between pirates and their supporters, and to look to INTERPOL as a guide in evidence collection.

INTERPOL's project BADA supplements the capacity of militaries engaged in counterpiracy activities to collect information that can be used for civilian prosecution of pirates. This has included support for information-sharing projects that share identifying information about suspected pirates (including pictures, name, nationality, identification documents, and biometric data) between the European Union and NATO.[17] INTERPOL has also worked to train investigators in the Seychelles looking into the financing of piracy, and is working with the shipping industry to develop their capacity to support evidence collection and preservation.[18]

The effectiveness of intergovernmental organizations is limited by their concerns over sovereignty. This concern leads them to reject mandatory demands from other international organizations—often they will only accept binding restrictions through treaties and conventions based on extensive negotiation and individual national ratification. Thus, the UN or its member organizations can make strong recommendations on courses of action and it can implore states to fund organizations working to address piracy but it must depend on the voluntary cooperation of states. This has left gaping holes in counterpiracy efforts. The best example of this gap, as discussed above, is that although the UN has urged states to criminalize piracy in their domestic codes, many states have not yet done so. Expressing frustration at this lack of action the head of the IMO, Efthimios Mitropoulos stated, "The political will has been pronounced by many people in positions of power many times, but this will is not being translated into deeds and acts."[19] Beyond problems of state compliance, the organizations themselves are often territorial and seemed to be more concerned with their own survival than with achieving end-state goals.

Regional intergovernmental organizations

Although piracy is a global phenomenon it is often managed at a local or regional level. Regional stakeholders have formed initiatives to address the specific dimensions of piracy in the regions where they live, sometimes with broader international support. This section discusses some of these regional initiatives in Southeast Asia and the Red Sea/ Indian Ocean region.

Before the world was focused on Somali piracy, piracy in Southeast Asia was the world's main hotspot. To address piracy in this region, the Regional Cooperation Agreement on Combating Piracy and Armed Robbery against Ships in Asia (ReCAAP) was signed on 11 November 2004 and came into force on 4 September 2006. Its three-pronged approach to suppressing maritime piracy includes: intra- and interagency information sharing and reporting; regional capacity-building; and cooperation with non-governmental organizations.[20] As of April 2011, there are 17 contracting parties to the agreement.[21] The IMO showcases ReCAAP as a model of regional cooperation because incidents of piracy dropped dramatically in the years 2004–6, although as of 2009 it shows signs of rebounding.

Central to ReCAAP is the Information Sharing Center (ISC) located in Singapore. The ISC focuses on information sharing, capacity-building, and cooperative arrangements.[22] Each contracting party/state has assigned a "focal point"—an organization, such as the navy, coast guard, or another designated agency to be the sole point of contact with the ReCAAP-ISC for that country. The focal points use a secure online information-sharing network to maintain around the clock links to each other as well as the main ISC in Singapore. Member states share information with the focal points, their partner organizations and the maritime industry "with a view to analyzing patterns and trends on the incidence of piracy and armed robbery."[23] The ReCAAP-ISC issues incident alerts and publishes regular reports to the public with analysis of the latest trends and severity of incidents of piracy and armed robbery at sea in Asia.

ReCAAP also arranges capacity-building workshops and has established several cooperation agreements with other intergovernmental and non-governmental organizations. The ReCAAP-ISC has established itself as the main authority on piracy in Asia by streamlining the reporting and information-sharing structure between Asian countries, offering training and support to those contracting parties who need to build their counterpiracy capacity and cooperate with like-minded organizations from various sectors.

While ReCAAP is a good example of regional cooperation, its role in the dramatic decrease in Asian piracy is less clear. Although the agreement was signed in 2004, it did not enter into force until 2006. Yet piracy rates in the region fell significantly between 2004 and 2006. It has been suggested that the tsunami in December of 2004, which destroyed many small boats and coastal villages, had a much more significant impact.[24] Another indication that ReCAAP cannot be credited with having a significant impact is that Malaysia and Indonesia, the two countries most affected by piracy, are not parties to the agreement and it was these two countries that experienced the greatest decrease in attacks. Finally, the ReCAAP-ISC's primary purpose was to improve incident response but in reality it does not play an operational role. As it is not the first point of contact when incidents occur, it is limited to gathering and disseminating post-incident information.[25]

The Malacca Strait Patrols, a set of cooperative security measures agreed upon in 2004 by the nations bordering the Malacca Strait, including Indonesia, Malaysia, Singapore, and (in 2008) Thailand may have had a greater impact. These agreements establish coordinated patrols, with each state patrolling its own waters. This program also includes an "Eyes-in-the-Sky"[26] initiative to provide coordinated aerial surveillance and the Sea Patrol Intelligence Exchange Group to coordinate information collection and distribution.[27] However, the limited number of flights operated by this program (two flights per week per country) greatly limits it effectiveness.[28]

The perceived success of regional cooperation in Southeast Asia catalyzed states along the Gulf of Aden and Indian Ocean to join forces to combat piracy as well. African Union initiatives to fight maritime piracy include the African Maritime Transport Charter,[29] the Durban Resolution on Maritime Safety, Maritime Security and Protection of the Marine Environment in Africa,[30] and Africa's Integrated Maritime Strategy.[31] In addition, the African Union participates in the Contact Group, the Djibouti Code, and the Regional Conferences on Piracy organized by the Eastern and Southern Africa – Indian Ocean countries. Through partner agencies the African Union works to establish a coast guard network in the region. The African Union also works to synchronize member state laws relating to maritime issues, and in the Durban Resolution called for member states to develop legislation that brings national law into line with international instruments relating to maritime security, such as the ISPS Code.[32]

On 29 January 2009, African and Arab states joined together to sign the Djibouti Code.[33] Its mandate is to create three monitoring and information-sharing centers—in Mombasa, Dar es Salaam, and Sana'a based on a focal point system. The three information-sharing centers were scheduled to be fully operational by April 2011 yet as of May 2011 only the Mombasa ISC has opened. In addition, a training center is being established in Djibouti.[34]

The purpose of the Djibouti code is to share information, interdict suspicious ships, ensure that piracy suspects are apprehended and prosecuted, and ensure that seafarers who have been harmed by pirates receive proper care. In addition to the four goals, each signatory agreed to work toward ensuring the criminalization of piracy in their domestic criminal code. Unlike ReCAAP, all the stipulations in the Djibouti Code are voluntary, and the level of actual commitment has been very modest, with funding for the implementation of the code of conduct coming from countries outside the region.[35] In addition, the initiative for establishing the Djibouti Code came from the IMO rather than the regional countries themselves, and while much progress has been achieved in terms of conducting legal reviews and initiating prosecution of suspected pirates in the region, it remains to be seen whether the Djibouti Code will become a self-sustaining organization in the long term.

The Intergovernmental Authority on Development (IGAD) originally developed by Eastern African states (in conjunction with the UN) to address famine and economic hardship in the region now addresses piracy as well. It is developing a plan to counter and prevent piracy as part of the overall regional strategy and regional action plan, focusing on inter-Somali dialogue and the internal development of Somalia as well as engagement with international groups. The overall intent is to address the root causes of piracy through locally developed solutions, and also to support regional states including the TFG in strengthening their control of their territorial waters and exclusive economic zones (EEZ).[36]

The previously mentioned organizations, however, are not the first attempts by African states to cooperate on maritime security. The Maritime Organization of West and Central Africa (MOWCA) was founded in 1975 and has 25 member countries. It is an intergovernmental institution for cooperation among various sectors related to maritime issues in West and Central Africa (including shipping and seafaring industries and groups working with maritime environmental issues and international conventions relevant to maritime interests). Its most significant project regarding piracy is The Sub-regional Coast Guard Network, a joint IMO/MOWCA project aimed at reinforcing information sharing, coordination, and cooperation between member states. MOWCA has not yet come into force because six of the 20 state parties have not yet ratified it.

The inherent difficulty faced by regional intergovernmental organizations is that it is difficult to get all regional parties affected by piracy to sign on to cooperative agreements. Although there is no requirement for regional cooperation on piracy in international conventions, the lack of full cooperation creates the potential for gaps in the coverage or enforcement of regional agreements. This difficulty affects both ReCAAP and MOWCA. MOWCA, for instance, is attempting to create a regional coast guard and yet without the participation of all the states in piracy-prone regions there will be areas of coastal waters that are not patrolled. ReCAAP as well operates without two key players in its region—Malaysia and Indonesia.

Cooperation within regional organizations is affected by territoriality and issues of national sovereignty. The naval vessels participating in the Malacca Straits Patrols, for instance, only patrol in their own territorial waters and cannot cross into neighboring states' waters. Practically this means that the naval vessel closest to a pirate attack may not be able to respond. It can only alert the neighboring state's navy, which may be too far away from the incident to do much good.

International military response

The navies are at the center of the international effort to counter piracy. They are tasked with protecting vital shipping lanes, arresting suspected pirates, collecting evidence, and transferring suspects to the countries that will prosecute. "International cooperation is the currency of naval power today," according to US Navy Admiral Gary Roughead, chief of naval operations. He continues, "These efforts confirm that there be no contradiction between defending our country's sovereign rights and sailing together against the common threats to our welfare."[37] As of the end of 2011, there are between 10 and 18 warships at any given time patrolling an area of about 1.1 million square miles in the Gulf of Aden and the Indian Ocean at a cost of approximately $2 billion per year.[38] This is a significant decrease from the start of the year despite an increase in pirate attacks. These warships represent three distinct efforts: NATO's operation called Ocean Shield, the European Union's Operation ATALANTA, and the multinational Combined Task Force-151 (CTF-151). These three efforts are assisted by navies from non-participating countries such as India, Iran, China, Russia, and Japan.

The North Atlantic Treaty Organization (NATO) has been engaged in counterpiracy missions off the Horn of Africa since October 2008. Its mission was to escort World Food Programme vessels to Somalia's coast. NATO believes it has a unique capability to bring a "comprehensive approach to counterpiracy efforts."[39] This comprehensive approach entailed assisting coastal states in bolstering their own naval capabilities, for example, creating their own coast guards. NATO's operations also include deterring and disrupting pirate attacks, rendering assistance to ships as required, and arresting suspected pirates. NATO also runs the NATO Shipping Centre website that provides piracy warnings and alerts including information about the location of sighted pirates. The EU Naval Force Somalia (EUNAVFOR) launched its naval operation, Operation ATALANTA in 2008. It began with a mandate to protect World Food Program vessels but soon decided to follow in NATO's footsteps and focus on regional development as well. Like the NATO mission, Operation ATALANTA protects global shipping, helps deter acts of piracy and armed robbery, and monitors illegal fishing activities off the coast of Somalia. As many as eight EU ships and a number of maritime patrol aircraft operate at any one time.[40] In addition to Operation ATALANTA, EUNAVFOR has established the Maritime Security Centre–Horn of Africa (MSC-HOA), which is staffed by military and merchant navy personnel and offers round-the-clock monitoring of vessels transiting through the Gulf of Aden.[41] On the ground, the EU provides military training to Somali security forces in Uganda in support of the TFG.[42]

In 2009, the US navy created the third multinational mission confronting Somali-based piracy. CTF-151's mission is to "deter, disrupt, and suppress piracy." Why the US navy felt it necessary to add a third multinational force is not clear although one theory is that while the NATO and EU missions offered a "Western approach" to piracy suppression, CTF-151 would offer an "Eastern approach."[43] This theory is supported by the fact that the mission has been commanded by Turkey (twice), Pakistan, and Singapore (twice). Countries that have participated in CTF-151 include Canada, Denmark, France, Germany, South Korea, The Netherlands, New Zealand, Pakistan, Portugal, Singapore, Spain, Thailand, Turkey, the United Kingdom, and the United States.

CTF-151 working with the US navy and the IMO recognized that most pirate attacks were occurring in the Gulf of Aden off the coast of Yemen. To deter these attacks and protect shipping in this vital seaway they established an International Recommended Transit Corridor (IRTC). The corridor stretches from the Bab al-Mandeb, a narrow strait separating the Red Sea from the Gulf of Aden 464 nautical miles to just north of the island of Socotra. The transit corridor is divided into several areas through which commercial shipping and private yachts are monitored by the various naval detachments. Although it is intended that naval vessels will escort ships of all nationalities to the IRTC, some navies will only escort ships in which their state has an interest.

It soon became apparent that a mechanism to coordinate these three international coalitions and the independent navies was required. The Shared Awareness and De-confliction (SHADE) initiative is an attempt to improve information sharing and reduce intraorganizational inefficiencies between the military groups operating in the Gulf of Aden and the western Indian Ocean. CTF-151 forces, NATO, and EUNAVFOR act as rotating co-chairs for meetings held every six weeks. Since the beginning in 2008, several other states, international organizations, and the maritime industry have joined the meetings. In addition to information sharing between militaries, these meetings also allow for discussion and exchange of views between various stakeholders affected by piracy.[44] Naming this organization SHADE, however, is telling— as neither "de-confliction" nor "shared awareness" is the same as cooperation.

Although the naval effort is extensive, it has not significantly reduced the levels of piracy and the pirates have proven resilient and adaptable. When the navies created the IRTC, for instance, the pirates simply moved their operations farther out into the Indian Ocean. Tasking the navies with disrupting pirate attacks in the 5 million square miles that comprise the Indian Ocean is beyond their capabilities. They are also hampered by inconsistent mandates and rules of engagement. The three naval missions give them little operational ability and navies are only allowed to arrest pirates caught in the act (which is very rare) or caught after the commission of an act of piracy.

Getting beyond the question of whether the mission is feasible, one must question whether having three separate international coalitions is efficient. A good example of this inefficiency is the fact that each naval force operates its own reporting center: The EU's MSC-HOA is in Northwood UK, the UK Maritime Trade Office is located in Dubai, and the US Maritime Liaison Office is headquartered in Bahrain. These reporting centers are in addition to the three regional Djibouti Code ISC, the IMB and the IMO reporting centres. Critics point fingers specifically at the EU/NATO rivalry saying that these organizations seem more concerned with proving their mettle than with fighting piracy off the coast of Somalia. NATO and the EU have a history of institutional rivalry and "at a time when both organizations are redefining themselves the current counterpiracy operations could be seen by both as an opportunity to carve out a new area of competence ... an edge that neither organization would want to concede."[45] But even if the naval coalitions were working together seamlessly they are hampered by political considerations. Most harmful to their mission is the lack of interest of their member constituents to prosecute the pirates that the navy arrests. It is estimated that navies release 90 percent[46] of the pirates they capture due to either insufficient evidence or the inability to find a state willing to prosecute them. Capacity and training also hamper naval efforts. Navies are equipped to fight wars. They do not generally train and equip their fleets to provide law enforcement. Naval vessels, large, slow, and supplied with heavy weaponry, are not ideal for the task.

Non-governmental organizations and industry

Non-governmental organizations, with their issue-specific knowledge bases play an important role in countering piracy. This section looks at the work of four non-governmental organizations: the International Maritime Bureau, the preeminent piracy data collection agency; the International Transport Workers Federation (ITF), which represents seafarers throughout the world; the Baltic and International Maritime Council (BIMCO), which represents the interests of the maritime industry; and Oceans Beyond Piracy (OBP), which convenes a working group of diverse stakeholders.

The International Chamber of Commerce established the IMB in 1981 to address maritime crime. Its primary initial focus was maritime fraud, but it has included a significant focus on piracy since 1992 when the IMB set up the Piracy Reporting Centre in Kuala Lumpur, Malaysia. This center provides a variety of services including a 24-hour emergency helpline for victims of piracy, an online piracy map, and a daily status report on piracy. The IMB claims to be "the world's premier independent crime-fighting watchdog for international trade" specifically because of its "multi-lingual and multi-disciplined staff, unique structure, industry support, and well-placed contacts."[47] Its most important task is providing up-to-date, round the clock information for shippers and law enforcement agencies throughout the world on pirate attacks through its Piracy Reporting Centre. The statistics it compiles on piracy incidents are used by agencies throughout the world. Even so it is estimated that most piracy attacks are not reported to the IMB.[48]

The ITF characterizes itself as a "truly global organization."[49] It serves as an umbrella organization for 780 unions, representing over 4.6 million transport workers in 155 countries.[50] Unlike some other organizations, which look at the economic costs of piracy, the ITF focuses solely on advocacy for seafarers, especially those transiting through dangerous waters. The ITF is particularly vocal in its fight against "flags of convenience," which it believes lower standards and wages for merchant mariners and significantly increase the likelihood of injury or even death. As Jon Whitlow, ITF Seafarer's Section Secretary, said, "The overwhelming interest of civil society is for the dissolution of the FOC [flags of convenience] system." The ITF, along with several other trade associations, sponsored a petition, signed by over 900,000 people to press government to do more to fight piracy and ensure workers' safety on the sea. They followed this up with the creation of a website (with assistance from several maritime industry groups), named saveourseafarers.com.

Unlike most of the organizations discussed previously, BIMCO makes a strong case that preventing piracy should not rely on solving governance issues on the ground in Somalia. As they write on their website, "The statements by government that the solution ashore remains the only solution to piracy is of little interest or use to the industry."[51] They reason that governance in Somalia will take some time but states cannot wait to take more robust action. BIMCO's most pressing concern is the inability of states to prosecute pirates and has lobbied governments to nationalize piracy codes. It also criticizes Western states for relying on governments in the Somali region to prosecute pirates instead of prosecuting pirates themselves. While BIMCO and other shipping interests press governments to do more to stop piracy, they staunchly resist any government regulation of their own practices, such as mandatory adherence to BMPs.

One other non-governmental organization is OBP,[52] which attempts to reduce the levels of piracy through better governance of the seas. It believes that to solve problems one must bring together the stakeholders affected by the problem. In the case of piracy these stakeholders include the shipping industry, the seafarers, governments in the regions where piracy occurs, and the international organizations that are working to suppress piracy. A key component of the project is the necessity of resolving conflicts peacefully. OBP plans on using a multi-step decision-making process which invites representatives from all areas affected by piracy to explore the problem and collectively develop specific, implementable solutions. The vision of the OBP project is of a coordinated, collective solution to piracy developed and executed by key actors across all the differing sectors affected by piracy.

Conclusion

On paper and in rhetoric the world understands that to combat piracy there needs to be a shared global effort. The problem appears to be that most organizations (in the piracy realm and elsewhere) are more concerned with their own survival[53] than advancing agendas or reaching solutions to their problems. In the piracy realm there is more "deconfliction" and "shared awareness" among groups than cooperation. Cooperation entails compromise yet many counterpiracy institutions zealously guard their turf instead of working together to achieve their goals. Instead of complementing their efforts organizations compete with one another. At least six different organizations,[54] for example, currently provide piracy warnings and new intelligence-gathering organizations continue to be created because existing organizations are not seen as functioning effectively, or because separate organizations value their autonomy so highly that they are hesitant to share information with others. Although unwelcome, piracy offers the world an opportunity to enhance global institutions and mechanisms that can both challenge piracy and foster cooperation on other global issues. The question is whether these institutions are up to the challenge.

4   Evolving norms and conventions

- Territorial seas vs free seas
- Human rights
- Conclusion

The contemporary response to piracy is different and more humane than responses in the past due to the fact that international actors accept new humanitarian and territorial norms. In this chapter we focus on two recent developments: first the idea that the sea is a common heritage of all and not a protectorate of some, and second the notion that all people—pirates included—are entitled to human rights.

Human understanding of the sea has evolved. Whereas people once regarded the sea as a "legal vacuum," in the twenty-first century many people view it as "common heritage of all mankind."[1] Some criticize this notion of "common heritage" as being without specific legal meaning, but for others it marks a turning point in the relation between states. After the treaty of Westphalia in 1648 the state became "the sole, legitimate actor on the world stage."[2] However, individuals within states began to see the need for "looking above the state to a multi-national sovereign in international crimes."[3]

Territorial seas vs freedom of the seas

Human society has struggled with various concepts of property rights not only on land but on the sea and in the air as well. Legal issues around property rights on land have been resolved, though not entirely solved, by the development of territorial states and their various ways of recognizing private property rights. Individual states differ in their conceptions of how private property rights are recognized and maintained, but these differences are generally not a global concern.[4] Recognition of property rights with respect to seas is a more perplexing problem. Resolving conflicts over sea rights has played a key role in the creation of international law. Whereas land can be occupied and garrisoned, rights to the sea, by its very nature, are more ephemeral and transient.

The nation-state is the primary actor responsible for providing a system for the protection of life and personal property rights on both the land and the sea. In its land territory, the state, primarily through its judicial system, has a near monopoly position, but this is not so at sea. For most of recorded history the protection of the maritime industry has been closely associated with states and sovereigns. The maritime industry is the only industry that has been an integral part of the development of international relations since recorded history began. This has created a significant place for the maritime industry in international norms and regulations. Codes of maritime conduct formed some of the first widely accepted international norms, going back to at least the time of the Babylonian King Hammurabi's Code (1700 BCE).[5] The *Lex Rhodia*, a code of maritime law developed by the island of Rhodes in about 800 BCE, appears to have been widely accepted in the eastern Mediterranean basin for a thousand years. The modern insurance practice of general averages, in which the various entities represented on a ship (cargo owners, shipper, etc.) share in any monetary losses incurred during hijacking, appears to be directly derived from the *Lex Rhodia*.[6]

The continuation of general averages over nearly three millennia is indicative of the traditional framework that still characterizes the maritime industry's laws, norms, and practices. Despite large changes in the organization and technology of the maritime industry in the last 50 years, the rigidity of the traditional regulatory framework has prevented commensurate changes in norms of the international regulatory structure. Amending international maritime regulations is a cumbersome, state-dominated process operating through multilateral conventions, treaties, as well as some of the intergovernmental organizations discussed in Chapter 3.

One difficulty has been that, according to international law, piracy takes place outside of a state's territory and therefore is of lesser importance to the state than their domestic concerns. In only a few instances, such as the skyrocketing cost of food in the Roman Republic at the time of Pompey, has piracy caused such acute disruption in society that it dominated the national political agenda.

Secondly, the modern international relations system, which is based on state sovereignty, has hampered solutions to piracy. For example, despite the legal development of universal jurisdiction, in the 1850s the

British government instructed their naval officers in the South China Sea to only involve themselves against Chinese pirates if British ships, cargo, or citizens were victims.[7] In this case the political repercussions of exercising universal jurisdiction over pirates were believed to be more severe than the problem they posed.

The overriding concern of states to maintain their sovereign privileges is as evident in the twenty-first century as it was in the nineteenth century. In 2010, UN secretary-general, Ban Ki Moon, appointed Jack Lang as a special advisor on piracy. In reporting back to the secretary-general, one of Lang's guiding principles was not to interfere with the sovereignty of Somalia.[8] In several resolutions, the Security Council has specified that foreign military forces can operate within the territorial waters of Somalia, and even against pirates on Somali land, but only with permission of the TFG.[9] Individual countries have had to negotiate their activities with the TFG, and only a few have done so. While discussed by diplomats and the media as though it were an extraordinary effort to stop piracy, these resolutions did not provide any unusual power—any country can give permission to foreign military forces to operate in their country, as NATO and Warsaw pact countries have done for years. It did more to help the UN promote the dysfunctional TFG, which maintains only 23 embassies[10] (the same number as Taiwan) as the national government of Somalia.

In a paradox of history, the norm in favor of all nations having a right to navigation through the "high seas" may be at an all-time high, when the accepted legal definition of what constitutes the high seas in international treaties is perhaps the most restrictive since the 1600s. The high seas have not always been open to all nations. While the concept of free navigation has been around since ancient times, it has been followed in its breach throughout most of recorded history. There have been attempts by sovereigns to claim territorial rights, or at least effective control, over parts of the seas. For example, with the participation of other European sovereigns, kings of Denmark extracted "sound tolls" for over four centuries from countries whose vessels wished to gain entry to the Baltic Sea. It was a practice that did not end until 1859.[11]

In some cases, such as with the Romans, Venetians, Portuguese, and Spanish, serious attempts were made to enforce claims of sovereignty over vast oceanic regions. Even the English kings claimed sovereignty over the four oceans surrounding England. The establishment of British admiralty courts was closely connected with the idea of the King's sovereignty over the British Seas. The King's peace needed to be kept on the King's seas.[12] The Dutch were required to recognize British maritime sovereignty over the British Seas in Chapter 4 of the Treaty of Westminster signed in 1674. Within those seas Dutch vessels had to salute the British flag.[13]

On the other hand, the oceans have also been seen as vast, trackless, and infinitely abundant territories that are beyond the ability of any nation to occupy or claim. In 1580 Queen Elizabeth of England, despite her claim to the British Seas, defended Francis Drake's foray into the Pacific by telling the Spanish Ambassador Mendoza that "The use of the sea and the air is common to all; neither can any title to the oceans belong to any people or private man, for as much as neither nature nor regard of the public use permitteth possession thereof."[14] Modern observers know that the resources of the ocean are not limitless, and our conceptualization of the sea is an uncomfortable mixture of national claims and freedom for navigation.

The seas can either be viewed as a shared resource and responsibility, as a free and essentially ungoverned area, or as national territory. In 1609 a Dutch jurist, Hugo Grotius, building on Queen Elizabeth's reply to Mendoza, formally set forth the principle of *Mare Liberum* (free sea) that no one state controls the sea and thus no state has exclusive jurisdiction over it.[15] Grotius, working for the Dutch India company, challenged the opposing principle of *Mare Clausum* (closed sea), in an attempt to pry the seas from Portuguese, Spanish, and English interests. *Mare Liberum* was not readily accepted. King Charles I of England asked the Dutch to punish Grotius, and any other Spanish, Venetian, and English authors who challenged the principle over the next half century, but the principle of free navigation gained strength. By the end of the seventeenth century navigation was practically free for vessels of all nations.

As a governance principle, the concept has certain problems. If no one entity has sovereignty over the seas, who creates and enforces laws for protection of life and property on the sea? Piracy was a case in point. By what right could sovereigns define an act as piracy if it occurred outside their territory? Who could enforce the rule, and under what authority could it be prosecuted?

As the British Empire grew, the British Parliament enacted several laws including the Piracy Acts of 1698, 1717, 1744, 1825, and 1837 that allowed pirates to be tried in courts established in any British colony. After the 1850s the colonial courts of the English, and other colonial powers, increasingly provided the legal institutions needed to criminalize piracy.

Even so, there were difficulties. China asserted that pirates caught within its territorial water were only subject to Chinese law. The English Governor of Hong Kong could arrest and try pirates caught on the high seas, and within the three-mile territorial limits of Hong Kong, but not those who fled into the territorial waters of China. Likewise, the English asserted that pirates caught in the British seas were subject only to English justice. In the early 1840's the British admiralty instructed Royal Navy ships not to attack suspected pirates unless British interests were involved and the attacks were directly observed. The result was an upsurge in piracy.[16]

For most crimes the state prosecuting the crime must have a connection to the crime—a nexus. This nexus demands that a crime is committed in their territory, or that a citizen, long-term resident (or their property) is the victim or perpetrator of the crime. Piracy, however, might be devoid of any of these bases for establishing nexus. The English partially tried to resolve these problems by further developing the concept of universal jurisdiction, which held that pirates were such a scourge on mankind that they could be tried by any state wherever they were found. In the absence of a consensus among states regarding universal jurisdiction, states lack judicial standing to bring particular pirates to justice if a connection with some breach of national law within that state's jurisdiction cannot be identified.

As discussed in Chapter 1, one of the first attempts to codify international customary laws or norms for piracy occurred at the International Law Project at Harvard University beginning in the 1920s.[17] The draft piracy convention pointed to a great deal of controversy regarding piracy. The difficulty, it claimed, was that "large scale piracy disappeared long ago ... piracy of any sort on or over the high sea is sporadic ... Piracy lost its great importance in the law of nations before the modern principles of finely discriminated state jurisdiction and of freedom of the seas became thoroughly established."[18] In essence, there was no contemporary consensus because the issue was nearly moot.

The group noted that piracy is traditionally a crime under state and not international law, but international law can provide the basis for extraordinary jurisdiction in every state to seize, prosecute, and punish the perpetrators. "The draft convention defines only the jurisdiction (the powers and rights) and the duties of the several states *inter se*, leaving to each state the decision how and how far through its own laws it will exercise its powers and rights."[19] The convention recommended giving states the right to prosecute the act of piracy occurring outside their territory, but not the obligation to do so. How far an individual state exercised that right depended on "the municipal law of the state, not the law of nations. It justifies state action within limits and fixes those limits. It goes no further."[20] The language used in the Harvard Draft Convention was taken almost verbatim into the 1958 Geneva Convention on the High Seas and later into UNCLOS, and is the most widely recognized legal definition of piracy in international law. The 1997 British Merchant Shipping Maritime Security Act also repeated the UNCLOS definition of piracy verbatim.[21]

UNCLOS (1984) and the Geneva Convention of the High Seas (1958)

For the purpose of piracy the two conventions can be taken together. The United States, which has not ratified UNCLOS, did ratify the Convention of the High Seas and thus has similar (although not identical) commitments as parties that have ratified UNCLOS with respect to piracy. The negotiating parties for these conventions largely considered piracy to be an archaic and nearly moot point. There was some reluctance to even include articles on piracy, but in the end the Harvard Draft Convention held sway.

The primary focus was on defining the economic and political rights of states over the seas and seabeds. While the 1958 convention started on this task, UNCLOS created several strong concepts of territorial waters, the contiguous zone, and the EEZ, but it was the development of the "transit passage" that permitted the stronger definition of territorial waters and the EEZ.[22] "Transit passage" was less restrictive than the more common term "innocent passage." In the territorial waters of states bordering international straits all ships, including military ships, enjoyed the right of transit passage. In particular military ships can maintain "normal modes of transit" which is taken to mean deployment of naval and air forces in a manner consistent with force security needs. Normal transit of a submarine may be submerged, which is not permitted in innocent passage. With the matter of transiting narrow waterways resolved, a consensus emerged that 12 nautical mile territorial waters was acceptable.

The convention gives a further demarcation of 24 nautical miles from a state's coast, calling it the contiguous zone. States had the right to police these waters and arrest criminals within this territory. Possibly the most daring part of the convention, however, was the designation of an EEZ which granted coastal states the exclusive right to the sea's resources 200 nautical miles from its shoreline. The United States would be the greatest beneficiary of this ruling. Its EEZ covers 3.4 million square nautical miles, an area greater even than its land mass.[23] The UN estimates that "87 percent of all known and estimated hydrocarbon reserves under the sea [and 99 percent of the world's fisheries] fall under some national jurisdiction as a result" of the creation of EEZs.[24] However, the contiguous zone and the EEZ were also considered part of the high seas for navigation purposes.

Although the convention gave a coherent framework to territoriality, the specific anti-piracy provisions of UNCLOS may not be seen as successful in establishing a universal prosecutorial regime, as discussed in more detail in Chapter 5.

SUA

A second, and more modern convention, SUA, directly addresses the problems associated with territoriality in arresting criminals at sea. For our purposes there are two ways SUA differs from UNCLOS. First, an arresting party must have nexus with the suspected pirates. Second, states can invoke SUA when a crime occurs within territorial waters as long as the hijacked or attacked vessel is scheduled for international transit. According to Article 4: "This Convention applies if the ship is navigating or is scheduled to navigate into, through or from waters beyond the outer limit of the territorial sea of a single State, or the lateral limits of its territorial sea with adjacent States."

Although SUA's main focus is counter-terrorism at sea, "the stated aim of the sponsoring governments was to produce a 'comprehensive' convention that didn't rest on existing distinctions [between piracy and terrorism]." As British Royal Navy Commander, Andrew Murdoch, writes, "It is important to note, however, that the word 'terrorism' appears only in its preamble. A terrorist motive does not form any express element of the crime set out in treaty."[25]

Again, unlike UNCLOS, SUA is binding in that each state party "shall" make the offences punishable. Further, it requires states that find suspects in their territory to prosecute or extradite them to another state that has established nexus to the crime. In article 11, paragraph 7 it stipulates that "all extradition treaties and arrangements applicable between states parties are modified as between state parties to the extent that they are incompatible with this convention."

States rarely invoke SUA, in large part, due to sovereignty issues. SUA permits states with nexus to reach into the domestic territory of another state. It largely does not depend on the municipal laws of another state to operate. It has been ratified by 156 states making it nearly as widely adopted as UNCLOS, but unlike UNCLOS, SUA has not achieved the force of customary international law.

Human rights [26]

Piracy was not the catalyst for the evolution of human rights norms. These norms were codified in the aftermath of the Second World War.

The perpetrators, the victims, and the bystanders of Nazi aggression were deeply scarred by the six years of world war. They emerged determined to safeguard individual human rights to mitigate the chance of such atrocities ever occurring again. Although this generation did not invent the notion of human rights they extended the circle of inclusion in those rights. Human rights would apply to victim and aggressor, law-abiding citizen and criminal. They were "one of the normative revolutions of our times."[27]

In previous eras, sovereigns considered pirates *hostis humanis* (the enemy of mankind) or *communis hostis omnium* (communities against all). The advent of human rights norms has allowed us to see the inherent dangers in this mindset. No one is outside of humanity—no matter what crimes they commit. Extracting individuals and whole communities from consideration as equal human beings is what leads to mass atrocities. The concept of universal jurisdiction, however, strips away the pejorative connotations of criminals as "others" while preserving the right of the states to arrest and try people for committing heinous crimes.

Human rights are not solely for the benefit of individuals, they advance societies. As legal scholar Bertrand G. Ramcharan writes in his book *Contemporary Human Rights Ideas*,

> Contemporary human rights ideas have a strategic mission: to rally the world around the belief that human rights are enabling and empowering, that human rights ideas are creative and foster development, that equality, development, and democracy can help build a better future, that gross violations of human rights sap the creative energies of humankind and impoverish us all ... [28]

Human rights norms and the conventions that codify them provide strict guidelines to states, including their navies and judicial systems, in the arrest, prosecution, and incarceration of suspected pirates. There are several human rights conventions that relate to the prosecution of pirates, some of which will be discussed below, but a fundamental expression of intent is the Universal Declaration of Human Rights (UDHR) adopted by the UN General Assembly on 10 December 1948. UN Secretary-General Ban Ki-Moon noted its importance saying, "The campaign reminds us that in a world still reeling from the horrors of the Second World War, the Declaration was the first global statement of what we now take for granted—the inherent dignity and equality of all human beings."[29]

The articles of UDHR most pertinent to piracy require that people are presumed innocent until proven guilty and that they have the right to a public trial. Further, no one can be convicted for an act which was not criminalized at the time the act was committed. Pirates therefore, must be dealt with exclusively through the criminal justice system of individual states. Killing of suspects is permitted only in self-defense if they violently resist arrest.

There are benefits beyond the immediate human rights benefits for treating pirates as criminals and not enemy combatants—it lessens the possibility of escalating violence. Eighteenth-century pirates of the West Indies became progressively more brutal as Great Britain began executing them with greater regularity. By the nineteenth century, the policy of executing pirates was well-established. Consequently, nineteenth-century pirates usually treated their captives much more harshly than did their sixteenth-century counterparts because they realized that it did not pay to leave survivors who might testify against them.[30]

Although there are many human rights conventions, the ones that impact counterpiracy efforts most are: the International Covenant on Civil and Political Rights (ICCPR),[31] the European Convention on Human Rights (ECHR)[32] and the Convention Against Torture (CAT) (see Table 4.1).[33]

Historically, human rights did not restrict state actions. States considered pirates both combatants and criminals "without the privileges or immunities of either class."[34] Eugene Kontorovich describes the status of pirates historically:

> [Pirates] could be tried when captured, unlike regular combatants, but if encountered on the high seas, they could be attacked and slain. Moreover, international law recognized that returning pirates to port for trial could be extremely burdensome, and thus it permitted summary shipboard proceedings and executions. In short, pirates had a status much like unlawful combatants: they could be dealt with either militarily or criminally at the enforcing state's convenience.[35]

Legal authority to detain suspects

By the mid-twentieth century international law and conventions clearly articulate the right of navies to arrest individuals caught in piratical acts. However, navies are not generally well-versed in the judicial and evidentiary nuances that attend the prosecution of pirates. In many countries coast guard or marine police units engage primarily in maritime law enforcement close to shore, and do not have a deepwater capacity. The US Navy has tried to adapt in dealing with Somali-based piracy. Each ship in the theater now has an officer or "legal detachment"

Table 4.1 Human rights conventions pertaining to piracy

Human rights convention	Issues addressed	Practical implications
Universal Declaration of Human Rights (1948)	"All human beings are born free and equal before the law." Right to fair trial by impartial tribunal. Presumption of innocence.	Suspects must be treated as criminals and not combatants. Cannot be harmed on high seas (unless in case of self-defense).
Convention against Torture and other Cruel, Inhuman or Degrading Treatment or Punishment (CAT)	"No circumstances of any kind, including war, may be invoked to justify torture." Non-refoulement to country where person subject to torture. Compensation by states for victims of torture. A committee of 10 experts monitors the implementation by state parties.	Although persons convicted of violent offenses can be refouled (or returned) to home country, Europeans are reluctant to do so. Transfer of prisoners to third-party states, such as Kenya, only when third party can guarantee fair trial, decent detention facilities, adequate food and medical attention.
1950 European Convention on Human Rights (ECHR)	Prohibits death penalty; right to be informed in one's own language of reasons for arrest and charges; right to fair, timely trial. Right to appeal guilty verdict.	Members of the EU will not enter into transfer of suspect arrangements with countries that have death penalty in their domestic code.
1966 International Covenant on Civil and Political Rights (ICCPR)	Prohibition on torture; right to fair trial.	

Source: United Nations and Council of Europe.

which trains the crew in the human rights laws and practices adhered to by the United States. Representatives from the US Coast Guard train the sailors who board the pirate vessels in rules of engagement and human rights. There is also at least one judge advocate general in the theatre who consults with all parties to ensure they abide by the stated rule of engagement and human rights obligations.

International law is not clear on how long a navy can hold prisoners on its ship before bringing them before a court. ICCPR Article 9 states: "Anyone arrested or detained on a criminal charge shall be brought promptly before a judge or other officer authorized by law to exercise judicial power and shall be entitled to trial within a reasonable time or to release."[36] In two non-piracy related cases, one involving a French navy ship which held prisoners for 13 days before bringing the suspects to port for trial and the other involving a Spanish ship which held prisoners for 16 days, courts ruled that delays are permissible under ECHR when unavoidable.[37] Under that standard, it is unclear whether naval vessels would have to leave the theatre to transport pirates as soon as they arrest them. Under the current system, it is likely that each national court would create its own answers.

A second concern is that navy ships are often not equipped with cells and other facilities for detaining prisoners. Penal detention may well involve the use of considerable manpower and/or excessive restraints. It is clear that under the current rules each national court would have to determine if the detention were unlawful and what consequences, if any, unlawful detention might have on a particular case.

Non-refoulement and torture (rules for transfer of prisoners)

Under both CAT and ECHR it is not enough for the receiving state to give "diplomatic assurance" to the transferring state that prisoners will be well treated. According to Amnesty International, "These promises are only sought from countries where international legal obligations to prevent torture and other grave human rights violations have not been respected ... If those countries do not respect those obligations, which are binding as a matter of international law, there are absolutely no grounds for confidence that they will respect promises given at a bilateral diplomatic level."[38] The Memoranda of Understanding (MoU) between the European Union (EU) and Kenya in which Kenya agreed to prosecute suspected pirates captured by the EU, cite the ICCPR and CAT. They also provide for post-transfer monitoring. According to the text: "Kenya will ... keep an accurate account of all transferred persons, including but not limited to, ... the person's physical condition, ... their place of detention, ... any significant decisions taken in the course of his prosecution and trial."[39] The EU also has the right to receive information about the prisoner in the event of declining health or any allegations of improper treatment and the right to visit and question transferred suspects. The MoUs explicitly rule out the possibility of a death sentence and require EU and seizing state representation at trial.[40]

Transfer itself is a thorny issue. It is based on Article 105 of UNCLOS, which grants the seizing state the right to prosecute. It does not however mention any right to transfer the suspects to a third party. Some scholars say the transfer is based on universal jurisdiction while others say that the framers of UNCLOS specifically worded the article in such a way as to avoid transfer to third parties. Nevertheless, the majority opinion holds that transfers accord with international law.

In the case of Somalia-based piracy, before the transfer of prisoners to Kenya could occur, the United Nations Office on Drugs and Crime (UNODC) refurbished a prison (to ameliorate overcrowding) and a court room for piracy suspects in Kenya. It also provided training in international maritime law for Kenyan lawyers and judges, and forensic equipment to the Kenyan police. MoUs were signed between transferring states to guarantee the humane treatment of prisoners.

Non-refoulement has made many Europeans hesitant about bringing pirates to their shores because they are afraid that once their jail terms are over it will not be possible to send pirates home. There is no basis for this fear as *non-refoulement* does not apply to violent criminals—there is no prohibition to return individuals convicted of serious crimes to their home countries. In Europe, individuals convicted of piracy are neither subject to the rules of *non-refoulement* nor are they eligible for asylum. This is not the case for those suspects found not guilty, however and while there is no legal restriction, popular sentiment will often, not allow deportations regardless of the suspect's innocence or guilt.[41]

Fair trial

In Article 14, the ICCPR lays out very clearly the rights to a fair trial that must be afforded to all detainees. These rights[42] are expressly guaranteed in the MoUs and include such things as the right to be presumed innocent, the right to counsel, and the right to a "competent, independent, and impartial tribunal established by law."[43]

The Kenyan judiciary, with help from the UNODC has gone to great lengths to comply with these stipulations. According to legal scholar, Douglas Guilfoyle:

> Despite the general backlog in Kenya's judicial system [the trials] commence promptly (in as little as six weeks), the pirates are represented by local lawyers (often with legal assistance), translators have been paid for by capturing states, EU-provided assistance has included "computers and money to bring more qualified judges to Mombasa" and diplomatic observers are routinely present.[44]

However, many municipal courts would have a difficult time maintaining these standards without considerable outside assistance. Even the more sophisticated legal system of Kenya does not normally provide defense attorneys to indigent defendants. The cost of this has been borne by outsiders. The cost of developing and maintaining such standards in a large number of countries, while perhaps desirable, would be very high. It is also not clear what liabilities states or individual officials might have should the MoUs be breached.

Opportunity for redress of transfer

According to Article 13 of the ICCPR, a person has the right to contest their transfer (known in legal circles as "effective remedy") to a third-party state:

> An alien lawfully in the territory of a State Party to the present Covenant may be expelled therefrom only in pursuance of a decision reached in accordance with law and shall, except where compelling reasons of national security otherwise require, be allowed to submit the reasons against his expulsion and to have his case reviewed by, and be represented for the purpose before, the competent authority or a person or persons especially designated by the competent authority.[45]

At present many transferring states have not institutionalized any mechanisms for ensuring the review of defendants' claims regarding transfer. This does not mean that they are necessarily in violation. The United Kingdom for instance does not have any official means of redress but has put defendant transfers on hold pending judicial review.[46] Still, states' non-compliance with this clause, for example in the transfer of suspects to Kenya, could put states in violation of their obligation under CAT and ECHR not to transfer suspects without the possibility of redress. States and individuals cooperating in piracy suppression efforts must meet their obligations under international human rights law lest they risk the nullification of prosecutions, potential liabilities in their own court systems or at the International Criminal Court, and international censure.

This discussion of human rights norms has emphasized the issues that are raised in the context of modern piracy. These issues are fundamentally tied to the view that pirates are to be tried in criminal state courts that may have universal jurisdiction. If this viewpoint shifts and pirates come to be seen once more as combatants or terrorists, as will be discussed in Chapter 5, then the legal basis that states use to engage with piracy will shift. Although combatants are entitled to fundamental human rights, the specific legal framework which governs their treatment is different.[47]

Conclusion

This chapter demonstrates the important impact of changing normative and legal conceptions of two issues key to piracy: what bodies have the responsibility for enforcing national or international law over the sea, and what limitations or restrictions should be placed on counter-piracy actors when they engage with pirates? In the first case, the generally accepted view in the modern era is that the high seas are a shared area outside the control of any specific state. This has created a gap of governance: if the seas are a shared commons, then there is no natural body or state with the responsibility to stop piracy occurring in this area.

Attempts to address this gap have taken the form of international agreements that define the responsibilities of states and where these responsibilities end, and establishing conventions to allow states to extend non-exclusive jurisdiction over the shared commons with respect to piracy. As discussed further in Chapter 5, these agreements establish a framework for the prosecution of piracy on the high seas, but the actual execution of this framework has been complicated by issues of capacity, concerns about sovereignty, and other political concerns.

The second case considered in this chapter has been the evolution of human rights norms and the restrictions they place on counter-piracy actors. Given this legal regime, those interested in eradicating piracy face two dilemmas. Since prosecutions are costly, just the legal right—and not a legal duty—to prosecute does not provide an incentive to prosecute, as the costs may be higher than the benefits. Many states decide to only prosecute pirates if their nationals are put at risk. Second, given the development of human rights norms and conventions in the twentieth century, there are significant challenges and unresolved debates about what legal and operational structures may work to suppress piracy while living up to the duty to protect human rights.

In examining the emergence of human rights and the multiple restrictions they place on state actions, it may be reasonable to ask if human rights norms now hamper anti-piracy efforts. Eugene Kontorovich writes: "the growth of international legal norms that limit state authority and provide greater protections for the individuals make it harder for nations to perform the oldest and perhaps most basic law enforcement function in international law: preventing piracy."[48] It is certainly the case that these developments pose historically novel challenges for navies and other groups operating to suppress piracy. However, this framing overlooks an important aspect of the development of human rights law over the twentieth century: it is now acknowledged both legally and normatively that human rights are fundamental and criminal prosecution systems need to adjust to ensure the protection of human rights. A criminal justice system that does not protect human rights is in itself a criminal undertaking. The question that faces modern counterpiracy operations is not how best to get around the restrictions that human rights laws and norms have placed upon them, but how to meet the legal and moral requirements, while still operating effectively to identify, capture, detain, and prosecute pirates on a sufficient scale to provide a deterrence to piracy.

In general, what we have found in the previous chapters is that the current framework for suppressing piracy consists largely of a nineteenth-century regulatory framework, implemented by twentieth-century institutions, trying to resolve a problem for an industry and world that has rapidly moved into the twenty-first century.[49] These changes in the legal and normative structures around piracy have created a variety of unresolved questions. Chapter 5 will address these current debates in more detail.

5 Current debates

- Piracy—a crime or an act of war
- Legal debates
- Tactical debates
- Conclusion

The evolving norms presented in Chapter 4 lead to certain vexing and contentious issues. In this chapter we examine these issues within three main issue themes: the question of whether states should treat pirates as criminals or combatants; the legal issues surrounding counterpiracy prosecutions; and the more tactical issues such as whether to pay ransoms.

Piracy—a crime or an act of war

As discussed in Chapter 1, Somali pirates have a clear business model that primarily seeks financial gain rather than political power. Although there have been rumblings of military prosecution, as of now, international law views pirates as civil criminals. As discussed throughout the book, states' perspectives on pirates have changed throughout history. Although currently the dominant perspective is that pirates are civilian criminals and subject to criminal prosecution rather than combatants subject to lethal military operations, there is no fundamental reason to believe that this is an immutable perspective. There is considerable pressure for states to take a more combative and militaristic stance.[1] The current section reviews some existing debates around this domain.

A fundamental question in the response to piracy is whether states should view pirates as criminals or combatants. Drawing from the historical analogy of the Barbary pirates, some commentators argue that piracy is a military issue requiring a military solution. However, this is challenged by the argument that most modern pirates do not meet the legal definition of lawful combatants. According to Douglas Guilfoyle writing on the specific case of Somalia, "the laws of war only apply during an armed conflict" and thus states may not treat Somali pirates as combatants because:

1. They are not involved in armed conflict.[2]
2. They do not knowingly attack foreign naval vessels.
3. They control no territory.
4. They have no military command structure.[3]

Many modern pirates do not seem to meet any of these criteria, and therefore should be subject to the legal system rather than military engagement. This is an important distinction because combatants can be the target of lethal force and criminals cannot. Criminals are legally designated as civilians and afforded basic rights, like the right to speedy trial. Conversely, assigning pirates the status of combatants would deny them certain rights such as due process, but would also allow them other rights such as using lethal force against those they deem their enemies.[4]

Proportionality is an important factor in state responses to illegal action. Piracy can be viewed as a crime that takes place on the sea in the same way as robbing a bank is a crime that takes place on land. One would not say that a bank robber is a combatant and in most countries one would not view this robber as someone the army should capture—it is a case for the local police force. Likewise, in the absence of the criteria that define combatants, pirates must legally be seen as criminals subject to police action and not military operations. Practically, whether this principle will hold if pirate attacks and the violence associated with them increase remains to be seen.

Are military strikes the answer?

History has shown us that military solutions have been used successfully as part of an overall counterpiracy strategy. Their success, however, was achieved through the allocation of massive resources. American folklore describes how in 1801 newly elected American president, Thomas Jefferson refused to pay tribute to Barbary pirates in exchange for safe passage through the Mediterranean. This refusal prompted a military offensive which lasted for four years and ended the practice of the United States paying tribute to the Barbary states. The story, however, did not end there. The truce only held for a few years when Barbary states once again demanded tribute. In the end, US military power did not stop Barbary piracy—the French occupation of Algeria in 1830 did. As stated in Chapter 1, piracy cannot exist in an effectively governed area and although the French occupation was not benign it did have the benefit of suppressing piratical activity. In the twenty-first century land invasion and occupation are much less acceptable options.

The idea of invading and occupying Somalia is even less appealing as a result of the US-led intervention in Somalia in the 1990s and the "Black Hawk Down" incident when 18 American and one Malaysian soldier were killed. There is little international appetite for large-scale incursion into Somalia.

The UN Security Council did give states the right to enter Somalia in 2008 and, with consent of the TFG, use "all necessary measures that are appropriate in Somalia ... consistent with applicable international humanitarian and human rights law," to stamp out piracy off the coast of Somalia.[5] The term "all necessary measures" allows the use of military force in Somalia's territorial waters and in Somalia itself. David Miliband, the British foreign minister, called this new resolution "an important additional tool to combat piracy. Any use of force, however, must be both necessary and proportionate."[6] Note, however, that this requires the consent of the TFG before international action is taken. Because of this, this resolution did not in fact create any new legal rights or abilities for international actors, but simply reaffirmed the position of the TFG as the legitimate government of Somalia.

Operationally, finding a military target is not difficult. Satellite imagery clearly shows pirate ports and even individual boats being fitted out for a pirate missions. It would not be hard to strike these ports or boats with missiles. International navies could also change their rules of engagement reflecting the view that pirates were combatants on a battlefield and use lethal fire from drones or direct fire as an option upon engagement, instead of trying to capture pirates for trial.

There are three main reasons, however, why military solutions are counterproductive. First, as discussed, there are legal requirements for individuals to be viewed as combatants. At the present time pirates do not fit into any of the current accepted legal standards.[7]

Second, military incursions will most certainly cause unintended civilian deaths. States often employ limited strikes as a means to deal with thorny foreign policy problems.[8] President Obama's counter-terrorism czar John Brennan emphasized the utility of limited force (although not addressing piracy in particular) in the summer of 2010 when he said, "We will exercise force prudently, recognizing that we often need to use a scalpel, not a hammer."[9] However, collateral damage in terms of human lives often undermines foreign policy objectives. According to Micah Zenko, fellow at the Council on For-eign Relations: " ... limited force is rarely as surgical or precise as one would imagine from Hollywood blockbusters or Pentagon YouTube videos. In reality, the intelligence used in targeting sites can be wrong, weapons systems fail, weather interferes, and humans routinely make mistakes."[10] Third, military strikes or land incursion would bring fur-ther misery to desperate people, and could very well be a catalyst for coalitions between pirates and insurgent groups operating in-country. Nothing builds solidarity like a common enemy, and military opera-tions can be an excellent recruitment tool for extremists. Military operations against pirates could take a vexing problem and turn it into a full-out war.

Max Weber once said, "every argument has its inconvenient facts."[11] This argument is no exception. As we saw in Chapter 2, states histori-cally defeated piracy by both offering a pardon and hunting down pirates and executing them before, or after, a trial if they refused the pardon.[12] What is stopping us from following history's example and simply doing the same? States do not follow this model because inter-national norms have evolved. In an attempt to safeguard what are now seen as basic human rights norms, international laws now draw a sharp distinction between combatants acting in war and individual criminals acting in defiance of the law. The widespread use of military tactics to deal with piracy is no longer seen as acceptable.

That is not to say that it is unacceptable to use military equipment and personnel to supress piracy. The military is often the only institu-tion with the requisite means to respond, and the only organization with the legal authority to respond under UNCLOS. This is part of the paradox of modern piracy suppression; the military is expected to respond, but may not use the combative military tactics they are equipped and trained to use.

Yet beyond a normative analysis, there is another reason why most states are not responding to pirates as combatants. As we discussed in Chapter 2 states historically treated pirates as enemies when they viewed them as predators—those who attack the authority of the state—and not simply as parasites.[13] In the early twenty-first century most maritime states view pirates as parasites while responding to those they consider terrorists as predators. If states perceive a greater threat level from pirates' action, they may indeed start classifying them as terrorists or combatants to be engaged by military force.

Such a shift is easily conceivable. Until the attack on the World Trade Center in 2011, the typical response to managing terrorism was a criminal response. Terrorists were tracked by police organizations, such as the FBI, arrested, and sent to trial. Almost overnight the United States' response to terrorism became a military response.[14] Senator Jim Webb (D-Va.) wrote: "Those who have committed acts of international terrorism are enemy combatants, just as certainly as the Japanese pilots who killed thousands of Americans at Pearl Harbor. It will be disruptive, costly, and potentially counterproductive to try them as criminals in our civilian courts."[15]

Is piracy terrorism?

This question is both ironic in that at the turn of the century terrorists were also considered criminals, and significant because a terrorist is now often viewed as an unlawful combatant. Unlawful combatants have limited, although existing rights, under the rules of war. Unlike lawful combatants who have immunity from prosecution for engaging in combat, unlawful combatants may be prosecuted for the crimes they commit.[16] In addition to piracy, they might also be charged with the war crime of intentionally targeting a civilian ship. The question is complicated by the fact that there is no internationally recognized definition of terrorism accepted by academics and politicians. Terrorism expert Bruce Hoffman describes terrorism as:

> fundamentally and inherently political. It is also ineluctably about power: the pursuit of power, the acquisition of power, and the use of power to achieve political change. Terrorism is thus violence— or, equally important, the threat of violence—used and directed in pursuit of, or in service of, a political aim.[17]

If we start from this definition, then piracy is not terrorism. Piracy is about theft or enrichment. Pirates may injure people in the commission of this crime but it is not their intent. However, other definitions of terrorism focus more on the targeting of civilians or on the role of terrorism as an instrumental behavior: threats or violent actions used with the intent of forcing a change in the behavior of others.[16] One could make the case that pirates who seize a ship, torture its crew, and force the ship owner or government to pay ransom fall under these definitions of terrorism.

Another part of the difficulty in determining whether piracy equals terrorism is the differing notions of what constitutes "private ends." UNCLOS article 101 states that "any illegal acts of violence or deten-tion, or any act of depredation, committed *for private ends* by the crew or the passengers of a private ship or a private aircraft ..." can be considered piracy.[19] But what are private ends?

One perspective is that "private ends" are financial or personal gains as opposed to political gain. If one adheres to this definition then piracy is not terrorism. Somali pirates and Southeast Asian pirates are clearly seeking money. Until recently the Nigerian case was more complex in that pirates represented themselves as members of politically motivated groups, but observers are now convinced that Nigerians are motivated by profit. However, another perspective argues that "private ends" means only that the act is committed by actors who are not affiliated with, or endorsed by, a state. Pirate gangs operating without the consent or cooperation of a state, but with political goals, could therefore fit the criteria for pirates and terrorists.

The Somali extremist group al-Shabab, if it follows through with threats to engage with piracy as a form of "sea *jihad*," may be a group that fits both definitions of terrorist and pirate.[20] This is particularly true if "private ends" only has to constitute a portion of the motivation for the act and not the entire act. Somali pirates who may believe they are protecting their waters from foreign poaching may, in part, have an altruistic purpose, but their collection and retention of ransom still makes their action piratical for private ends. The meaning of "private ends" was taken quite expansively in the case of *Castle John v NV Mabeco*, where in 1986 a Belgian Court of Cassation ruled that a Greenpeace vessel had committed an act of piracy when it attacked a Dutch vessel. This court held that the Greenpeace vessel had been acting in support of a "personal point of view," not a political one, during the attack.[21]

An irony of this debate is that most of international law treats terrorism as a crime. Existing UN treaties on terrorism, such as SUA or the 1971 Convention for the Suppression of Unlawful Acts against the Safety of Civil Aviation all focus on the criminalization of terrorism.[22] Even UN Security Council Resolution 1373 (2001), passed in the wake of the September 11 attacks on the US, calls on all states to:

> 2(e) Ensure that any person who participates in the financing, planning, preparation or perpetration of terrorist acts or in supporting terrorist acts is brought to justice and ensure that, in addition to any other measures against them, such terrorist acts are established as serious criminal offences in domestic laws and regulations and that the punishment duly reflects the seriousness of such terrorist acts;

Inded, on 2 October, 2001 British Prime Minister Tony Blair said to the Taliban "surrender the terrorists; or surrender power."[23] It was the perception in the West that the Taliban, then Afghanistan's recognised government, refused to treat the Al-Qaeda suspects as criminals and were instead giving them safe harbor. That made the state complicit in the attacks and legitimized the war against the State of Afghanistan for permitting its residents to harm another state. It is not at all clear that treating pirates as terrorists would permit the military to take a more combative stance. In fact, treating terrorists (as in the first instance) as combatants is legally troubling.

Legal debates

Although piracy has a long-standing relevance to the legal system, as discussed in Chapter 4 there are still challenges around the definition and appropriate judicial response to piracy. One question is whether piracy is a particularly heinous crime and worthy of universal jurisdiction. Legal scholar Eugene Kontorovich demurs from the conventional wisdom by suggesting piracy does not rise to the level of a heinous crime as do the other crimes that merit universal jurisdiction, such as genocide and crimes against humanity.[24] This argument is dismissed by others, who argue that state practice, which is considered the "best indication of customary international law demonstrates that universal jurisdiction for piracy on the high seas," is an accepted practice.[25] Indeed, piracy is the archetype for universal jurisdiction from which other crimes of universal jurisdiction claim root. The current section reviews some other open legal questions.

Are transfer agreements legal?

The United States, the United Kingdom, and other states have signed Memoranda of Understanding with states in the Indian Ocean region, including Kenya, the Seychelles, and Mauritius. These agreements allow an arresting navy, generally from a wealthy country, to transfer pirates they've captured to regional states for trial and incarceration. Although the arresting states have the naval resources to capture pirates, they have little interest in trying the suspects on their home territory. European states, in particular, are fearful that upon their release from prison pirates will stay in the country as permanent residents. Although legally states have little to fear—pirates would not qualify for asylum or non-*refoulement*, Europeans are reluctant to return people to a place where they are in danger.[26] The transfers are based on Article 105 in UNCLOS which states:

> On the high seas, or in any other place outside the jurisdiction of any State, every State may seize a pirate ship or aircraft, or a ship

or aircraft taken by piracy and under the control of pirates, and arrest the persons and seize the property on board. The courts of the State which carried out the seizure may decide upon the penalties to be imposed, and may also determine the action to be taken with regard to the ships, aircraft or property, subject to the rights of third parties acting in good faith.

Some question whether this clause permits transfer agreements.[27] They interpret the clause, "The courts of the State which carried out the seizure may decide upon the penalties to be imposed," to mean that *only* those states that seize the pirates can try them. They also argue that transferring is not a legitimate "penalty" because prison conditions are generally far worse in the receiving countries.

A majority of the legal proponents of transfer agreements under UNCLOS argue that "nothing on the face of the article makes the jurisdiction exclusive to the arresting state. Instead, it is permissive."[28] The arresting state *may* try the suspects. Alternatively, proponents of transfer agreements argue that nothing in international law prohibits states from making bilateral treaties. If an international treaty does not explicitly forbid an action, consenting states can make any sort of agreement that does not conflict with other international law. Ultimately, these are questions of legal interpretation and will not be settled until actors with the legal will and capacity bring cases around these issues.

A stronger case for transfer agreements might be based on SUA, which allows prosecution where "the alleged offender is present in its territory."[29] SUA also states that "The master of a ship of a State Party (the 'flag state') may deliver to the authorities of any other State Party (the 'Receiving State') any person who he has reasonable grounds to believe has committed one of the offences set forth in article 3."[30] Once the suspected offender has been delivered to the receiving state, he will be "present" in its territory and be prosecutable. Because SUA has not normally been used against piracy,[31] this is one area where states are not utilizing the tools available to them.

Venues for prosecution [32]

Leaving aside the question of military prosecutions (which will be discussed more in Chapter 7), theoretically, pirates can be tried in three types of civil courts: domestic, regional, and international, although at the moment domestic courts are the only courts authorized to do so. Universal jurisdiction allows for any country to prosecute accused pirates regardless of a nexus to the piratical act. While each venue has both drawbacks and merits, there is no single determinative factor which makes one venue superior to others. While expediency dictates one venue be employed by states for the prosecution of pirates, it is conceivable that a combination of venues would be used as is suggested in the sections below.

Domestic courts are the national courts, or more properly the municipal courts, of a given state.[33] According to UNCLOS municipal courts are responsible for piracy cases. And because most piracy emanates from the developing world, much of the domestic prosecution has taken place in developing countries such as Kenya and the Seychelles. These domestic prosecutions raise questions: are judiciaries in the developing world equipped to deal with complex issues of international law? Will they respect human rights? Does the state have sufficient resources to collect evidence, provide defense counsel for accused pirates, and incarcerate pirates in safe, sanitary jails?

In the case of Kenya, states, through the UNODC, have assisted the Kenyan government by training personnel involved with pirate prosecutions, from judges to jailors. They have also provided Kenya with the resources to upgrade court and prison facilities. Essentially the Kenyan criminal justice system is being leased by states. This "lease" can be (and has been) broken at Kenya's will.

There are some suggested reasons for prosecuting pirates in domestic courts of neighboring states. They include: ease of evidence collection and witness testimony; trials conducted by individuals of common heritage and in a common language; and lower costs because domestic prosecutions are generally less expensive than regional or international trials.[34] Thus, although there are certainly drawbacks to conducting piracy prosecutions in the domestic courts of states closest to piracy outbreaks, there are potential benefits for making them work.

Some legal scholars believe that a better venue for prosecution would be a regional court. Presently there are no regional courts in existence with the jurisdiction or competence to adjudicate piracy prosecutions. Moreover, there is no international custom or convention to make states responsible for neighboring states' actions. However, two factors make a compelling argument for regionalizing piracy prosecutions. First, while we argue in this book that piracy is fundamentally a global governance problem, the severity and individual characteristics of piracy vary regionally. The drivers and nature of piracy crimes can differ greatly. In Somalia, for instance, it is the lack of effective governance and economic opportunity that is motivating piracy, while in Nigeria it started with political grievance and evolved into greed.

Second, states have an interest in regional security that is compromised by piracy crimes, and similarly the economic impact of piracy can be dramatic at the regional level. Regional tribunals can be constituted by several states in a region acting together and given jurisdiction over the entire region. A Somali court sitting in Kenya and using Kenyan judicial facilities, as suggested in the Lang report[35] could be another model. A hybrid tribunal built within a given domestic judiciary of one or more countries in partnership with international organizations with jurisdiction over regional issues would be another. It utilizes a mixture of domestic and international law,[36] and employs both domestic and international judges. Either may offer a solution that would combine the benefits of domestic and international tribunals, while minimizing their respective flaws. Both are difficult to create as funding sources and harmonizing laws and procedures would take time to develop. Hybrid courts add judicial talent, support personnel, and financial assistance to domestic judiciaries to create a mixed entity. By enhancing domestic tribunals in this manner, rather than replacing them, hybrid courts can allow states to retain a stake in prosecuting crimes that would overwhelm domestic tribunals working alone. This characteristic helps make hybrid tribunals an appealing forum for the prosecution of region-specific crimes. By integrating international resources and expertise into domestic judiciaries, hybrid tribunals allow the states to bolster the effectiveness of regional states in upholding the rule of law, rather than simply taking over the work of prosecution or funding prosecuting nations.

This enhancement of existing judiciaries is particularly relevant for Somali piracy, as a lack of well-developed judiciaries in the region has increased international demand on those few states with functioning judicial systems to hear piracy cases arising in the region. The "strength" or "weakness" of a given tribunal for piracy prosecutions is, at least in part, related to an arresting nation's ability to rely on that tribunal's ability and willingness to prosecute captured pirates. By combining the political will to prosecute of an individual state with the expertise of international judges, hybrid tribunals would present a strong forum for piracy prosecutions.

A third venue option is an international tribunal with global reach. There are two potential courts already in existence that may be appropriate for piracy prosecutions: the International Criminal Court (ICC) and International Tribunal of the Law of the Sea (ITLOS).

The ICC was established in 2002 upon the ratification of the Rome Statute by a sufficient number of states. The court currently has jurisdiction over the crimes of genocide, crimes against humanity, and war crimes. Piracy, by definition under UNCLOS, is an illegal action that takes place in international waters. The international ramifications of piracy are seen in the victims including shipping companies, ship owners, and crew members, all of whom are likely to be of different nationalities.[37] It is also the case that piracy has significant international follow-on effects to people not directly affected by acts of piracy through its impact on world and local economies. For all these reasons, it is possible to make a legal argument that the appropriate jurisdiction for piracy would be found in international courts such as the ICC.

A particularly compelling argument for the use of the ICC in piracy prosecutions is its complementarity to domestic prosecutions. The ICC already has a regime in place by which it exercises jurisdiction over an offense only when the state having jurisdiction fails to investigate or prosecute.[38] This regime coincides well with the concept of state jurisdiction contained in UNCLOS, but suffers from the fact that UNCLOS did not make piracy an international crime subject to international prosecution but a national crime subject to extended jurisdiction. SUA does create certain acts of maritime violence as an international crime, and its extradite or prosecute clause would be supported by complementarity. From a technical standpoint, adding piracy to the jurisdiction of the ICC may be relatively simple because the court already exists and procedures are in place for amending the Rome Statute which establishes the jurisdiction of the court.[39] Politically, however, it would be much more difficult as states are reluctant to add any treaty crimes to the ICC's jurisdiction and piracy is not even a treaty crime.

Another international venue is ITLOS. While not designed to handle criminal prosecutions but rather disputes between states, ITLOS could, with some manipulation, make a potential international forum for prosecuting pirates.[40] This could take the form of ITLOS as an advisory body to domestic courts dealing with complex legal issues concerning the Law of the Sea. The advice of the tribunal could be binding and in this way international legal bodies would have ultimate authority over piracy prosecution. After all, ITLOS being comprised of jurists whose expertise is the Law of the Sea and having been formed by UNCLOS, may be best situated to interpret the treaty. This position would require extensive reworking of ITLOS's current focus and the purpose with which it was created, which could be problematic.

Can a judicial response act as a deterrent?

The best venue for trying pirates is an important question to consider. But a basic question may be more important. Can the threat of trial and incarceration act as a deterrent to the individual who considers whether to set out to sea? Existing research on deterrence theory suggests that in the case of piracy, legal deterrence may not have been strong. Deterrence theory suggests that punishment must be severe, certain and swiftly applied.[41] The international effort as of 2011 seems unable to meet these basic deterrent requirements. It is common knowledge that even when caught in the act, most pirates will be released by the arresting navies. For example between 22 August 2008 and 11 July 2010, only 28 percent of pirates arrested at sea went to trial.[42] The special advisor to the UN secretary-general gave a more startling statistic. According to his report of January 2011, "more than 90 percent of pirates captured by states patrolling the seas will be released without being prosecuted."[43] This suggests that deterrence has not been tried in the present form. Legal deterrence is not a factor in the current response to piracy. If the structure of enforcement and judicial operations were changed so that the four criteria described above were met, it is possible that this could change.

There is another interesting factor at work. Societal norms have an important effect, and researchers have argued that a large proportion of the deterrence effect of laws comes from the fact that they merely reflect existing social consensus.[34] Take for instance two efforts to stop transnational crimes: slave trading and the so-called "war on drugs." The British had success in stopping and eventually abolishing the slave trade because their populace had turned against the practice and began to see it as immoral. The war on drugs conversely has been a failure due in large part due to social acceptance of illegal drugs. This suggests that an important part of the legal system is to reflect and potentially influence social attitudes. If the communities from which piracy emanates view piracy as acceptable, or necessary, they will not be part of an effort to stop it.

Tactical debates

The previous sections focused on philosophical and legal disagreements. In this section we discuss four "tactical" or lower-level operational points of contention including: whether the global response can be successful if it focuses on the sea and ignores the land issues; whether merchants should protect themselves by hiring armed guards; whether shippers should pay ransoms to free their crew; and whether international actors are using the piracy problem to further geopolitical ends.

Should we increase the focus on land issues or concentrate primarily on the seas?

The current global effort to counter Somali piracy focuses its efforts off the coast of Somalia and in the Gulf of Aden and not on the land. Although Somalia (through the TFG) receives significant international aid through programs such as the World Food Program, international interest in direct military intervention has been low since the 1994 pull-out of US forces.

A consensus is emerging that unless the root causes of piracy are addressed, the crime will continue and intensify. Roger Middleton, Chatham House researcher specializing in the Horn of Africa summed up the current state of affairs this way: "The most powerful weapon against piracy will be peace and opportunity in Somalia, coupled with an effective and reliable police force and judiciary. Containing or ignoring Somalia and its problems is not an option that will end well."[45] According to former US naval officer, James Wombwell, "If you eliminate the shore havens or modify the political conditions that make piracy possible, then piracy will die out. If those pillars remain intact, then no amount of naval patrols are going to fully suppress piracy."[46] But while the importance of addressing the root causes on land is not controversial, it is also not simple. States throughout the world have thus far been stymied by repeated, failed efforts to stabilize Somalia.

Recently, however, approaches to non-military actions on land are emerging. One of the most innovative plans is from Bronwyn Bruton, an expert on Somalia. She calls on the United States to forge a new path, one that "lessens American involvement in Somalia without giving up on the objective of undermining al-Shabab and denying al-Qaeda a sanctuary."[47] She calls this policy "constructive disengagement." Acknowledging the counterintuitive nature of her idea, she contends that "doing less is better than doing harm, and there are good reasons to believe that the results will be more successful."[48]

She explains that al-Shabab, a brutally repressive insurgent group that has taken over much of southern Somalia, is not as cohesive as many observers believe. Rather it is "an alliance of convenience" that would fracture given time and the right conditions. She believes that the United States should create these conditions by "disengaging from any effort to pick a winner in Somalia, and by signaling a willingness to coexist with any Islamist group or government that emerges, as long as it refrains from acts of regional aggression, rejects global jihadi ambitions, and agrees to the efforts of Western humanitarian relief agencies in Somalia."[49]

The next phase of her plan involves waiting until anti-Western sentiment subsides and only then re-engaging. Re-engagement entails encouraging local economic development but does not involve pressure for centralized state-building. Bruton acknowledges that constructive disengagement "entails risks" but she warns that "the alternatives are far more dangerous."[50] She concludes that " ... ineffective external meddling threatens to prolong and worsen the conflict, further radicalize the population, and increase the odds that al-Qaeda and other extremist groups will eventually find a safe haven in Somalia."[51] Even if this approach is successful, it will take time to come to fruition. While it is developing merchant mariners face the question of how they should respond to the threat of piracy. One question they face is whether to arm themselves or not.

Should merchant vessels be armed?[52]

As governments and organizations try to determine the best way to put an end to hijackings, the question of whether or not to arm the crews of merchant vessels is inevitably raised. Proponents argue that armed mariners could prevent pirates from boarding their vessels. The mere presence of weapons aboard merchant vessels might deter attacks by making these vessels less appealing targets. Opponents of arming merchant ships identify several concerns with this approach, including the chance of an escalating arms race and increasing the likelihood of violence.

Arming merchant vessels against the threat of pirates is not without historical precedent. Historically, merchant vessels were well armed. The East Indiaman, for instance, a class of merchant ship used by various European countries from the seventeenth through nineteenth centuries was designed to carry significant armaments to defend ships against pirate attacks. If modern merchant vessels were armed it might be possible to prevent pirates from boarding.

Many modern merchant vessels are easy targets for pirates. Large oil tankers, for example, are slow moving and when laden down with cargo have easily surmountable freeboards. Compounding the problem, heavily automated ships often carry small crews composed of the bare minimum number of seamen required to operate the vessel. While this yields greater profits for shipping companies, it also means that pirates have a much easier task in gaining control of the vessel.[53]

An alternative to arming the crew is to hire private security guards. This approach has met with success in the past including the April 2009 defense of an Italian cruise liner by Israeli armed guards.[54] After pirates seized the *Maersk Alabama* on 8 April 2009, precipitating the dramatic rescue of Commander Richard Phillips, Maersk decided to employ armed security. The decision paid off. A few months later, pirates once again attacked the ship. This time private security responded with small arms fire and successfully repelled the attack.[55] Ideally, all the security detail needs to do is fire warning shots to deter the pirates. The goal is to "deter the attack rather than to engage and capture the pirates."[56]

The fiercest critics of arming merchant vessels are often the unions representing the seafarers. The fear among many seafarers' unions is that arming crews would expose them to greater violence. In the Somali case, pirates have not generally killed the hostages as this would complicate ransom negotiations. Arming ships could lead to firefights in which mariners are very likely to get hurt or killed. Moreover, there is the practical question of where private security guards could be berthed onboard the ship: in many ships, there may not be sufficient crew quarters to augment the crew.

Critics also contend that arming crews would cause an arms race with pirates. In the words of the managing director of the Hong Kong Shipowners Association, "If we arm our crews with light machine guns, [the pirates] can probably buy heavy machine guns. And if we buy rocket launchers, they can buy heavy ones."[57] Given that ransoms have given many pirates deep pockets to purchase weapons, it is a race that could go on indefinitely. Arming crews on vessels with flammable or explosive cargo is particularly dangerous. A stray bullet on a ship carrying chemicals or gas could quickly turn the ship into a fireball resulting in catastrophic loss of life and environmental devastation.[58]

Trained security guards aboard merchant vessels might relieve the crew of the burden of using weapons to defend themselves, but this, too, carries its own problems. There are no clear rules of engagement for these guards and no entity to which they are accountable. It is not clear that the Master of the ship could control the guards if a firefight broke out. In Nigeria there are reports of private guards, who are all provided by the military, acting with impunity and killing suspected pirates at will, with no one to stop them. According to journalist John Burnett, "this is as wild west as it gets." He describes a conversation he had with the head of a private security company operating in the Niger Delta:

> "You see bodies floating ashore regularly," Winchester says. "I'm in favor of rough justice"—and then *sotto voce*,—"too much paperwork as it is. We try to be as humane as possible, but there is a degree of ruthlessness involved. If you have to teach someone a lesson it has to be something they will remember."[59]

In March 2010, one such private guard killed a Somali pirate attacking the vessel on which he was stationed. As Arvinder Sambei, legal consultant for the UN, said of the incident: "There's always been concern about these companies. Who are they responsible to? The bottom line is someone has been killed and someone has to give an accounting of that."[60]

Trade unions and ship owners are also concerned about potential legal issues surrounding the presence of weapons onboard ships when they are in harbor. Most states do not allow arms to enter their territory. Some states will allow a private security firm to enter territorial waters but require that port officials confiscate the weapons while the ship is in port. Egypt, for example, decided to prohibit weapons from transiting the Suez Canal. Their policy required that security personnel hand over weapons upon entering the canal. Egyptian port officials then return the arms as the ship is departing the canal. These practices may violate national and international laws on the trafficking of small weapons. The varying and inconsistent laws around weapons in ports, and the potential for serious legal consequences to those who violate them, raise questions about whether a legal environment exists that would permit more active self-defense by merchants.

Should ransoms be paid?

The primary economic driver of piracy in Somalia is the ransoms paid for ships and crew. Therefore, a reasonable argument is that if no ransoms are paid, the economic equation will shift. However, refusing to pay ransoms could expose hostages to significant violence.

The amounts paid to Somali pirates in ransom are reaching new heights, with no end in sight. The large amounts paid out will likely increase the number of attacks. An ordinary Somali earns $600 per year, whereas a Somali pirate can earn over $10,000 in a single raid.[61] Given this discrepancy, it is easy to see why the payment of ransoms would encourage Somalis with little economic alternative to go into piracy, increasing the amount of piracy overall. There is also evidence that the ransom payment model has fueled similar acts of piracy beyond the Horn of Africa. The well-publicized ability of Somali pirates to obtain large sums for their captives may have contributed to the rise of piracy in Nigeria and South America.[62]

The question of whether or not to pay ransoms is complicated. Initially, paying ransom can be economically efficient. When ransom demands are relatively low, shippers can absorb them into their operating costs. However, there reaches a point when this "cost of doing business" is no longer economically feasible to the shipping company.

Currently the ransom price seems to be rising without a ceiling to contain it. Ransoms paid to Somali pirates have increased from an average of $150,000 in 2005 to $5.4 million in 2010.[63] In May, 2011, Somali pirates received a $13.5 million ransom for the release of a Greek supertanker, the *Irene SL*, three months after it was hijacked. There is no doubt that this latest payment will further incentivize hijackings among Somali men who likewise seek their fortune. Once pirates seize a ship, the navies will generally not board it for fear of injuring or killing crew members. This leaves only one avenue for the safe release of the crew and cargo: negotiating a ransom. It is the ransom negotiation that keeps the crew safe and it is in the Somali pirates' best interest to make sure hostages survive. Although certainly not an ideal situation at least "for right now it is a predictable business transaction."[64] When states deviate from this model, the transaction becomes less predictable. The Indian Navy, for example, raided a pirate mother ship and have also arrested over 100 other suspected pirates in recent years. In retaliation, pirates refused to release all of the Indian crew remaining aboard the *MT Asphalt Venture* even after receiving the ransom payment.[65] This action can also be seen as threatening violence against civilians in order to influence the behavior of the Indian government and turning at least this gang of pirates into terrorists.

The Nigerian model is "notable for the willingness of pirates to use violence."[66] If ransoms are refused to Somali pirates, they could well shift to such a model that similarly minimizes the value of the lives of the hostages they capture. Unless politicians find new ways of combating piracy the shipping industry believes it has little option other than to pay the ransoms. The problem with ransoms is that they form the working capital of the gangs, potentially fueling the purchase of more significant weapons and equipment and increasing the danger to seafarers. Furthermore, no one has been able to track the money and there are fears that ransom money is being diverted to terrorist groups to support their activities.

Does geopolitics influence counterpiracy measures?[67]

While the world powers may portray their counter piracy actions as a limited effort to suppress maritime piracy, others fear they are using the piracy threat as a cover for other national security goals. They are concerned that defending against piracy provides an excellent justification for the redistribution of naval and other military assets. It appears that some states have increased their naval presence, not so much to deter pirates, but to protect important oil trade routes and to act as a check on the growing naval presence of rival states.[68]

There are positive and negative impacts of these apparent balance-of-power actions. Some policymakers suggest that balance-of-power politics will facilitate more alliances on maritime security issues. Opponents believe that it will hamper the progress of counterpiracy operations because states, always sensitive to the protection of their national sovereignty, will fear other states' growing influence near their territorial waters. China, for instance, is wary of American involvement in the Strait of Malacca because of the proximity to the Taiwan Strait. China views this involvement as a move in support of Taiwan's independence and against its 'One China' policy. They have a reason to be concerned—some analysts agree that the United States is using piracy in the Strait as a cover to gain a foothold in Asia. The theory goes that the United States is trying to move itself into a more prominent role in the region to counter an increasingly powerful China and deal with any future security threats, such as a conflict over Taiwan.[69] While China is wary of American interest, India is concerned about China's growing military influence in the Indian Ocean.[70]

Worldwide energy consumption is expected to increase by 49 percent from 2007 to 2035.[71] Protecting important choke points, such as the Strait of Malacca, is an important consideration among both minor and major powers. States fear that an increased naval presence by other nations under cover of countering maritime piracy could be redeployed to hinder energy access through important straits. About 80 percent of China's oil comes through the Straits of Malacca, making the free transit of this area a critical national security interest.[72] China's naval strategy has prioritized maintaining a presence and power projection capabilities across the sea lanes that its oil transits.[73]

In the end, as much as they celebrate naval cooperation, navies from India, China, Russia, and elsewhere may be as much rivals as they are allies.[74]

Conclusion

The current chapter discussed some issues that are seen as "hot topics" in the area of piracy and counterpiracy operations. Piracy, as both a historical and an evolving phenomenon, poses significant questions of how international and national bodies should respond. This leads to debates and open questions at the legal as well as tactical level. In the next chapter, we develop the analysis of these open questions to address some more fundamental challenges: not just the question of what debates remain to be resolved, but what fundamental gaps in governance allow piracy to flourish in the modern world.

6 Key gaps and criticisms

- Coastal and flag state failure
- Legal gaps
- Political gaps
- Capacity gaps
- Conclusion

Piracy occurs when governance on land and sea are weak or where coastal states neglect their responsibilities. This neglect may be willful if state officials benefit from piracy or it can be involuntary if the state does not have an enforcement capacity. The failure of governance mechanisms is the reason that piracy has been able to rebound in the twenty-first century. There are also several second-order gaps that exacerbate the challenge of counterpiracy work. Gaps in the legal framework hamper more robust arrest and prosecution of suspected pirates. Gaps in the knowledge of how to fix failed states and gaps in international relations that permit failed states to exist make identifying the best policy difficult. Lack of capacity for naval enforcements creates opportunities for pirates to attack merchant vessels with near impunity. After a discussion of governance failures in coastal and flag states we focus on these secondary gaps that further exacerbate the problem. In the end, we find that the majority of responses to piracy are haphazard and focus only on secondary gaps while ignoring the root causes of piracy both at the local and global level.

Coastal and flag state failure

Historically, the primary defense against piracy has been responsible coastal states. Under international law, it is the state's responsibility to prevent predatory behavior by their citizens on others and the use of their ports by pirates. Most coastal states effectively prevent piracy by prohibiting pirates from equipping boats, acquiring heavy weapons, and setting out in the first place. When this fails, states patrol their waters with a coast guard or marine police unit and respond to suspicious behaviors. They prohibit and interdict the sale of pirated loot, the holding of hostages, and the use and laundering of ransom payments as a part of their criminal justice system. It is important to make the distinction that most countries do not prohibit the payment of ransoms by private individuals or organizations. They do not criminalize the conduct of the victims, but rather criminalize the use of ill-gotten gains by the perpetrators.

The impact of shore-based governance is significant: piracy only flourishes where shore-based governance systems are weak, and efforts to enforce governance directly impact piracy. Overall, dependence on the coastal states to suppress piracy has been remarkably successful.

The impact in local areas demonstrates the capacity of states to control piracy. In 1984 and 1985, Nigerian authorities committed significant customs, police, and naval resources to gather information on pirate bases. With the information gained, they raided the bases and the pirate markets for stolen goods, depriving them of their safe havens. The result was a dramatic drop in piracy in 1986. However, the commitment was not sustained and piracy returned to high levels again by 1988. Similarly, Somali piracy was significantly reduced during the rule of the Islamic Courts Union in areas under their control.[1]

The abdication of this responsibility to prevent piracy from developing can be driven by a simple lack of capacity on the part of the government, or it can be supported by the active collusion of members of the government for reasons of personal profit or political motivations. In the modern context, many scholars of Somalia suggest that members of the regional or local governments may be sharing in the significant profits generated by pirates, and hence may be less motivated to use what capacity they have to suppress piracy.[2]

The perception of the local population is also a key factor in creating safe-havens for pirates. As Chapter 2 demonstrates, if locals support pirates by sheltering or doing business with them it enables them to continue their activities. Ultimately, however, no matter the reason for the gap, piracy first and foremost results from the failure of the coastal state and communities to prevent their nationals from committing acts of piracy. The near quadrupling of independent states since 1945 has created international recognition of weak states that are either unwilling or unable to meet their obligations to control the predatory behavior of their citizens on international maritime traffic. While Somalia is the most egregious example, states around the Gulf of Guinea, in the South China Sea, around the Bay of Bengal, and elsewhere have also shown inconsistency and weakness in controlling predatory activity emanating from their ports. In some cases we have seen, such as the Philippines and Indonesia, domestic insurgency or rebellion supporting a portion of the domestic population that does not accept the internationally recognized government as legitimate, has undermined a state's ability to control ports in particular regions. In the past, this reluctance or inability of a sovereign to control piracy was a cause for war. Numerous wars throughout history have been initiated in order to protect a sovereign's merchant fleet from pirate activity.

If the coastal state is the first line of defense against pirates, the flag state, historically, is the next. In the twenty-first century, however, the flag states do not have the capacity to fill this role, creating a gap in the traditional second line of defense as well.

Under international treaty, the flag state has a particularly significant role in maintaining the rule of law on the high seas. Historically, states projected their municipal laws onto the sea through their flags as discussed in Chapter 2. The laws of the flag state apply to its ships and its courts have the right to prosecute crimes committed under or against its flag. Historically, there have been strong connections between the state of registry and the owners and crew of ships. A country's trade was often dependent on its own vessels to carry goods to foreign markets. The farmers, traders, ship owners and crewmen could collectively exert strong political influence to ensure that their country protect them, and the countries with which they were flagged were maritime powers with the capacity to follow through with their responsibility to protect the ships from pirate attacks.

The development of open registries in the second half of the twentieth century[3] has broken this historical link. Now, most of the world's merchant fleet no longer flies the flag of a maritime power—a state with the diplomatic, judicial, financial, and military capacity to protect mariners and enforce existing piracy rules. Unlike the past many ships are now commanded and crewed by citizens from a variety of states, perhaps none of whom are from the state of registry. Furthermore, the cargo is no longer necessarily arriving or departing the state of registry or any of the crew's states. It is entirely possible for a ship owned by a Danish company but flagged in Liberia and staffed with Filipino crew to be carrying goods from China to the United States when they are attacked by pirates. The ultimate result is that a country's trade is no longer dependent on the use of its own ships, and consequently there is a political separation among those having the power to enforce piracy suppression measures, those having the responsibility to suppress piracy, and those suffering most from the pirate attacks and hostage taking. The role of the US Navy in current counterpiracy operations demonstrates this well—the United States, in the interest of protecting global trade in the abstract, has several ships participating in counterpiracy activities off the coast of Somalia. The commitment of these ships is contingent on other regional needs, however, and instability in the Middle East and other national security concerns have caused the redeployment of ships away from counterpiracy operation.[4] However, when pirates have captured American nationals on American-flagged ships, the United States has deployed significant forces to interdict the specific ships, rescue the hostages, and bring the pirates to justice.[5]

Most of the flag states have little or no political or economic accountability in the welfare of their flagged ships or their crews, and virtually no capacity to respond. The naval powers also have little political accountability for the foreign flagged merchant ships or their foreign crews providing them with little incentive to intervene. The ship owners also lack the legal authority and means to protect their vessels. While owners may have a legal responsibility for their crews, they have no political influence in their crews' home states and often only a limited amount of authority in their own countries. By tradition, ship owners expect states to protect them, but it is unclear in the twenty-first century which states have a vested interest and capacity to help.

The failure of a coastal state to prevent its shores from being used by pirates is a failure to project its power over its own territory, and to govern its territory at a level sufficient to meet its fundamental obligation to other states "to ensure that its territory is not used in any manner which would disrupt the political, economic and social stability of another State."[6] There is a gap between the performance of the coastal state and the expectations for performance by other states. There is also an expectation that the state that is most affected by piracy is the flag state, whose "territory" is attacked by pirates. However, the shift to open registry flag states means that it generally does not suffer the political, economic, and social disruptions as much as the states whose citizens are held hostage, robbed, or killed, or the states whose commerce is interrupted, or the state of the owner whose property is held for ransom. Thus, there is a second gap between the expectations (expressed in conventions such as UNCLOS), of flag states to defend their ships and to extend the rule of law over their ships, and the actual capacity and performance of open registry flag states.

These fundamental governance gaps are systemic and have enabled the development of piracy in the twenty-first century. However, there are additional gaps in law, politics, available resources, and knowledge that further hamper the ability of states, and non-state organizations, to suppress piracy. We address each of these domains in turn.

Legal gaps

There are several problems in the prosecutorial realm that create complications and legal gaps in the judicial response to piracy. Most significantly: 1) UNCLOS is not binding on states; 2) the international conventions that guide the current effort were written at a time when the levels of piracy were believed to be so low that most of the framers thought the problem had largely vanished from the world scene; 3) international institutions and laws have not kept pace with evolving norms; 4) piracy is a global problem and yet each state has its own definitions and laws to fight it without any overarching structure to ensure complementarity or enforcement; and 5) international law defines piracy as occurring on the high seas although many acts of piracy occur in territorial waters.

As discussed in Chapter 4, the language used in UNCLOS is non-binding and merely provides for extended jurisdiction over piracy, allowing each state to seize pirates and to determine the penalties to persons and property so seized. The convention does not make piracy an international crime nor proscribe any international venue for prosecution or penalties for those convicted of piracy. While it declares that "All states shall cooperate to the fullest possible extent in the repression of piracy on the high seas or in any other place outside the jurisdiction of any State,"[7] the convention imposes no specific obligation on any state to enact laws against piracy. This is in contrast to other articles in UNCLOS. For example, the language found in UNCLOS Article 113 that discusses "The Breaking or Injury of a Submarine Cable or Pipe Line," begins with "Every State shall adopt the laws and regulations necessary to provide that the breaking or injury by a ship flying its flag ... shall be a punishable offence."[8] The articles on piracy could have begun with a similar admonition to require every state to adopt laws and regulation to make piracy on the high seas a crime punishable in its courts but they do not.

The legal framework for piracy has many shortcomings stemming in part from the fact that the framers of UNCLOS and the conventions that preceded it wrote the laws when piracy was not a major global problem. In 1924 the League of Nations refused to put piracy on their agenda stating that "it is perhaps doubtful whether the question of piracy is of sufficient real interest in the present state of the world to justify its inclusion in the programme of the (proposed) conference ..."[9]

Although those advocating for inclusion of piracy in the law of the sea had more success in later conventions, laws on piracy were never much more than an afterthought. Piracy was continually viewed "first and foremost as a historical phenomenon rather than an acute or potential threat."[10] During the 1958 convention, delegates debated whether to address piracy at all. The Czechoslovakian and Albanian delegates proposed limiting the discussion on piracy to one article which would read: "All states are bound to take proceedings against and to punish acts of piracy, as defined by the present international law, and to cooperate to the full possible extent in the repression of piracy."[11] These delegates argued that giving piracy more than a brief mention would "be out of all proportion for the present draft to contain eight articles dealing with an eighteenth century concept."[12] However, other delegates disagreed, and those in favor of including the eight (out of 320 total articles) articles prevailed. The resulting eight articles define the legal framework that is used to regulate piracy. It is interesting to note that the single paragraph proposed by the Czechoslovakian and Albanian delegates which binds states to "take proceeding against and to punish acts of piracy" might actually have been a stronger and more effective declaration than the eight articles used.

The timing of the writing of piracy laws is important for another reason as well. The world has changed considerably since these laws were written and they do not reflect current realities. In the twenty-first century changes in the structure of the merchant marine fleet and increasing trade between countries have meant that piracy is truly global in its impact. Yet the authority to prosecute piracy still resides with each state and its domestic laws. Not every state has anti-piracy laws in its national code. Of the states that do have piracy codes many are centuries old. The United States, for instance has not updated its piracy statutes since 1846. Since independence in 1947, India had not adopted any piracy codes and recently had to rely on British colonial laws to prosecute pirates.[13]

Although international law grants jurisdiction to any state to seize pirates, as anticipated in the Harvard Draft, the state must also confer onto itself the jurisdiction to arrest and prosecute.[14] The IMO's secretary-general summarizes the problem in a 2009 speech:

> ... relatively few national legislations exist fully incorporating the definition of piracy as contained in article 101 of the United Nations Convention on the Law of the Sea (UNCLOS), as well as a jurisdictional framework based upon the concept of universal jurisdiction regulated by UNCLOS; and that, in most cases, piracy

is not addressed as an independent, separate offence with its own jurisdictional framework but is subsumed within more general categories of crimes, such as robbery, kidnapping, abduction, violence against persons, etc. In such cases, prosecution and punishment can only take place in accordance with a jurisdictional scope that is inevitably more restricted than the scope of universal jurisdiction regulated in UNCLOS.[15]

The legal framework that addresses piracy is also hindered by the lack of harmonization in piracy laws among states. Penalties for piracy range from capital punishment in Yemen, to mandatory life sentence in the United States to a few years' incarceration in the Netherlands. As discussed in Chapter 5 this lack of harmonization in states' domestic laws hampers the deterrence effect. UNCLOS does not require states to harmonize their laws. It merely defines piracy and authorizes states to seize and prosecute.[16]

Perhaps an even greater pitfall in UNCLOS's reliance on states is that in an effort to respect states' territorial sovereignty UNCLOS defines piracy as occurring only on the high seas.[17] UNCLOS is silent on the legality of such acts within territorial waters. The presumption must be that such acts are jurisdictionally the problem of the state in whose territorial waters they occur. The problem with this approach is that most acts of piracy (as defined in Chapter 1) occur in territorial waters such as straits of international importance. Article 100 does not even impose a duty to cooperate in suppressing piracy occurring in territorial waters. Adding to the problem is that UNCLOS has added millions of square miles to territorial waters by expanding the state's territorial waters to 12 miles. The maritime industry is left with legal recourse to only those governments least able to arrest and prosecute pirates. After all, piracy only occurs systematically near those countries that allow the operation of pirates in their territorial waters. Meeting this challenge requires states to be robust and concerned enough to have enacted domestic laws under which armed robbery at sea is a crime and to have committed resources to enforce those laws. For the reasons cited previously this is not often a priority for new and weak states.

While UNCLOS clearly defines territorial issues it is vague on other important questions. It defines the intent to commit piracy as tantamount to the act of piracy but it does not define what constitutes intent.[18] Legal scholars such as Eugene Kontorovich argue that the possession of certain equipment whose only use is for piratical acts should be sufficient to establish intent. He cites nineteenth-century efforts to stop the transatlantic slave trade in which certain articles aboard a ship necessary only for transporting slaves, such as a large quantity of leg irons, were sufficient evidence to detain and prosecute suspected slavers.[19] In the Somali case, he argues that boarding ladders, RPGs and/or other heavy weapons with explosive shells—that is, equipment necessary only for piracy—should be sufficient evidence for arrest and prosecution. UNCLOS provides navies the authority to board ships with suspicious equipment but they must depend on their municipal law in determining if they have sufficient grounds to arrest and turn the pirates over to civilian courts for prosecution. Without clear municipal laws navies generally release suspected pirates at sea or on shore. It is also important to note that even if states included equipment articles in their piracy codes it might not prove to be effective as pirates generally dump their weapons and equipment overboard when approached by a naval vessel.

UNCLOS is also vague on the issue of incitement. Article 101 includes in its definition of pirates "those who incite or intentionally facilitate an act of piracy." Yet the article does not define these terms. We can assume that actions such as funding or organizing piratical efforts would constitute incitement and facilitation, but we are again left with each state creating its own definition or, more typically, not creating such a crime. Even if Article 101 did define these terms it does not give states any rights to arrest or prosecute because these are activities that are likely to occur within the domestic territory of a foreign state. The convention only gives states the right to arrest and prosecute such persons when they are on a vessel controlled by pirates.

The limitations of UNCLOS prompted states to develop a second convention, SUA, to fill some of the known gaps. While from the perspective of counterpiracy enforcement SUA is an improvement over UNCLOS because it allows states to prosecute violent attack on ships even when it occurs in another state's territorial waters. Moreover, unfortunately, states where piracy is prevalent, such as Thailand, Malaysia, Somalia, and Indonesia have not ratified the convention.[20] It is rarely invoked despite the fact that 157 states have acceded or ratified it.[21] This failure to invoke SUA may suggest that states currently view territorial sovereignty as a more pressing concern than piracy.

Scores of legal scholars have spent significant time examining the legal framework of piracy prosecution in an attempt to bolster it, and the gaps identified in this section represent some of the most commonly identified problems with the current international legal structure. It should be noted that an alternative perspective is that these gaps are not the main drivers of problems with the prosecution of piracy. Some scholars argue that international law gives states all the tools necessary to prosecute. The real problem, they argue, is that states do not believe it in their interest to prosecute suspected pirates especially when they have no connection to the piratical act. In essence, many argue that the real gaps are not legal, but political. These political gaps are in large part the result of open-registry flag states.

Political gaps

Underlying the response to piracy is the fundamental question of whether states believe it in their interest to tackle piracy. On the one hand, it is an insulting question: many states have exerted significant efforts to address piracy. However, one of the themes of this book is that to truly address piracy, states and non-state organizations need to work together to develop a global solution to this global problem. Yet, states seem reluctant to turn counterpiracy rhetoric into action.[22]

Concerns over national sovereignty and national security make many states reluctant to allow foreign forces into their territory to suppress piracy. Unsettled territorial claims in many parts of the world, particularly in Southeast Asia where conflicting claims from China, Taiwan, Vietnam, the Philippines, Malaysia, Indonesia, and Brunei for various island groups, make the deployment of naval patrols to suppress piracy, a delicate foreign policy matter. Even absent territorial disputes, countries are suspicious of the projection of military might by traditional rivals. Again in Southeast Asia, any projection of power by the Japanese, Chinese, or Indian navies is regarded with deep suspicion by each other and by many of the smaller states.[23]

National security concerns also lead many states to oppose merchant ships carrying armed guards and lethal weapons. They are concerned that permitting armed security details on vessels would give terrorists and pirates an opportunity to move about posing as armed guards. It could also increase the risk to government personnel engaged in legal interdictions, encourage arms smuggling, and create a greater risk from illicitly operated vessels. Countries where gun ownership is strictly controlled, such as England, view armed merchant mariners with alarm.

Fiscal concerns may also inhibit full cooperation in counterpiracy regimes. While states may have a theoretical interest and the amorphous international obligation to protect ships and their crews, it is expensive to maintain the infrastructure and institutions necessary to patrol, investigate, detain, try, convict, and punish pirates. Establishing an effective piracy control system, particularly one that meets the procedural considerations of international justice, is difficult and costly.[24] The immediate, high cost of protecting what are often a small group of foreign owners, insurers, and seafarers, may provide little direct benefit to states. Allocating resources to prevent piracy has to be weighed against the use of those funds for other domestic concerns. In democratic states, the public may not support such expenditures in the national budget, particularly when the pirates, as they often do, claim some altruistic reason, such as a religious calling, fisheries protection, or nationalism to justify their acts.

Finally, the level of concern regarding piracy, expressed by some of the more developed parts of the world—Japan, Europe, and the United States—juxtaposed against the high cost of effective anti-piracy efforts by regional developing countries can lead to conflict of interests. Some developing countries have found that permitting a certain amount of piracy has been rewarded by an increase in foreign assistance from the developed countries. It is often argued that economic hardship is the cause for piracy, and foreign assistance is the cure.[25]

Capacity gaps

Key actors may have the political interest and legal authority, but simply lack the apparent capacity to act. A major demonstration of this capacity gap is found in the problem of coastal states: if piracy is best eliminated by preventing safe havens on land, the global coalitions should be able to address piracy by working with states where piracy is endemic to improve their capacity to govern. In Southeast Asia this strategy largely worked because the littoral states have "functioning governments that were open to international persuasion and assistance."[26] Cooperation between littoral states and outside states (especially after the 2004 tsunami) along with the presence of naval vessels providing aid to victims, and the destruction of pirate boats helped reduce piracy in the area.

Those working in the counterpiracy field know that the key to reducing piracy is to stabilize weak coastal states—the end goal is clear and uncontroversial. The problem is that states and industry have a limited capacity to positively influence the domestic politics of weak or failed coastal states.

In part this limited capacity points to a gap in knowledge about fixing weak and failed states. No global power or institution has figured out how to bring stability to failed states. In the early 2000s for example, the US government toppled a violent dictatorship in Iraq and a militant theocracy in Afghanistan to bring freedom and democracy to their people, yet the situation years later is that both countries are arguably neither free nor stable. Even in what might be considered success stories—Kosovo and the Balkans—international forces are afraid to leave lest the previously volatile situations re-ignite. This gap in knowledge is exacerbated by the fact that the proliferation of new states in the last half century has also created more opportunities for state failures and unstable environments in coastal states where piracy can flourish.

Foreign affairs expert, Fareed Zakaria has written that the difficulty in fixing failed states is that "the odds of success are low and the risk of unintended consequences is very high."[27] He warns that it may not be realistic to "fast-forward political modernization, compressing into a few years what has taken decades, if not centuries, in the West."[28] In Somalia for instance the United States initially engaged in 1992 as part of a US mission to avert famine but after the famous Black Hawk Down incident it withdrew. Years later, fear of an Islamic takeover of the country by the Islamic Courts Union prompted the United States to intervene again. This time it began funding rival Somali factions and backed the Ethiopian military invasion. The result of the invasion was the loss of many lives and the emergence of a new faction called al-Shabab, which is more violent and radical than the Islamic Courts Union. As Bronwyn Bruton argues, "We have a limited capacity to influence events in Somalia, to influence them positively, but we have an almost unlimited capacity to make a mess of things."[29]

Bringing governance reforms to Puntland and southern Somalia is a monumental task. After 20 years of effort, many lives lost, and billions of dollars from stakeholders such as the UN, Western powers, and regional governments, the solution is nowhere in sight, and indeed it can be argued the situation has gotten worse. The Western world does not know how to create stable countries that are both domestically and internationally responsible.

Unlike the situation in Somalia, a government exists in Nigeria, but massive corruption at all levels of government allows piracy to flourish. Nigeria is not a poor country, although most of its people are very poor. The Nigerian constitution calls for 13 percent of the oil revenue to be directed toward the states from which it is extracted.[30] Yet, this doesn't happen. Piracy and kidnapping in the fishing industry, against foreign offshore oil facilities, and in its harbors is rampant. It appears to have some benefit to politicians jockeying for resources and power. Pirate gangs are offered political protection, as the crime is almost never prosecuted. Intervention in Nigerian politics or foreign patrols of territorial waters are not permitted by the government.

In both cases, other states' respect for the countries' sovereign rights, despite the countries' failure to meet their national and international responsibilities, prevents the direct elimination of pirate havens. Despite billions of dollars in outside assistance and economic aid, poverty remains endemic in Nigeria and Somalia. Crime and corruption on shore are rampant. The impact of Nigerian anti-piracy activities demonstrates that strong coastal states, with vigorous enforcement, can be a key part of stopping piracy. However, political challenges have so far made this a difficult criterion to accomplish.

Along with the lack of knowledge in fixing failed states there are other gaps in capacity as well. The world's navies, for instance, do not have the means to complete the counterpiracy mission in the Somali arena. Commodore Michiel Hijmans, commander of NATO's Ocean Shield compares the task to policing on land: "It's a huge area, almost twice the size of mainland Europe (close to 20 million square kilometers), and we are trying to patrol that with 20–25 police cars, which is a hell of a job."[31] According to Colonel Richard Spencer, British chief of the EU's naval forces, patrolling it would take "five times as many ships as the task force can muster."[32] Even with the support of aircraft, most of the area has no naval presence at any given time. Colonel Spencer acknowledged that a naval response is not the answer—"the military resource is finite and only treats the symptoms. We're only holding the line."

Another capacity gap involves the littoral states, which in many ways have the most to lose in piracy epidemics due to the exposure they have to the threats of pirates, as well as the disruption in trade that pirate activity in their region may bring. States that border Nigeria and Somalia, for instance, have limited naval and judicial capacity. Some of these states do not even have coast guards and even when they do, they are not up to the task of providing law enforcement off their coasts.

Bringing criminals to justice is a cornerstone of modern law and thus a judicial, prosecutorial response to piracy is vital. But the regional states of East Africa currently, and will for a long time, lack the capacity to deal with the epidemic of piracy. While there are an estimated 1,500–2,000 Somali pirates, Kenyan courts are strained to capacity with just over 100 cases. Many of their judicial systems are also weak: lawyers and judges do not have adequate training in international maritime law, they are backlogged with domestic criminal cases, and they do not have adequate prison facilities.

Many analysts believe that in the absence of states' ability to prosecute the most effective venue for piracy cases is an international court. It also makes sense because piracy is an act that directly affects global interests, and is often committed in the global commons of the high seas. As discussed in Chapter 5, some legal scholars would like to see the ICC expand the jurisdiction to include piracy. These analysts feel that "It is a gaping omission that the Statute of the International Criminal Court (ICC) has not given the court jurisdiction over piracy. This is especially poignant when it is realized that not every state has the facilities for such trials and those which do may not be willing to go through the trouble" to prosecute.[33]

However, piracy was not the only omission, and the court was not given jurisdiction over piracy for solid reasons. First, piracy in UNCLOS is not a crime under international law, so its inclusion would have been problematic. Second, even under SUA, where acts of violence at sea are a crime, it is only one of many "treaty crimes" created by various international treaties. The draft of the Rome Statute of the ICC originally included treaty crimes, but the practical problem of dealing with the issues of treaty crimes and how to handle non-acceding states, caused them to remove all treaty crimes from ICC jurisdiction. To have retained them would have made ratification of the founding statutes difficult. Moreover, while piracy was a problem, it was not perceived to be an international crime of the same magnitude as genocide and crimes against humanity. It was not in keeping with the ICC's mandate to deal with anything but the most egregious offenses and would have trivialized the court.[34]

UNCLOS did establish ITLOS, which sits in the "Free and Hanseatic City of Hamburg."[35] It would be historically sentimental for a piracy court to sit in a Hanseatic city, since as discussed in Chapter 2 the Hansa was established in 1241 to help protect merchants from pirates. It would also seem appropriate for a court established by UNCLOS to enforce the rules in the treaty against piracy. However, ITLOS was not established to be a criminal court and the convention does not give the court jurisdiction over pirates. Therefore, there is no international court with the jurisdiction to try piracy and it would be difficult and time-consuming to create such a venue.

Conclusion

Piracy flourishes when a coastal state is either unwilling or unable to prevent it. In past eras the flag states were better able to protect global shipping even when coastal states could not. In the twenty-first century there is no second line of defense and this gap leaves mariners and the shipping industry vulnerable. A more robust system is difficult to develop because changes in the ownership patterns of ships and the countries of registration over the last 50 years have considerably reduced the political importance of the maritime industry in the states that have the military, fiscal, and judicial resources to address the problem.

Significant legal challenges surround the definition and prosecution of piracy as well: the restrictive definition of UNCLOS and the more expansive but less utilized definition found in SUA both fail in either theory or practice to provide a comprehensive, useful guideline for identifying which court has the authority to prosecute pirates. In addition to these challenges, states face a fundamental question of whether piracy is significant enough to justify the devotion of adequate resources to the problem, and when these resources have been devoted they have overwhelmingly been on the naval front—what Martin Murphy has described as "the least efficient and cost-effective form of piracy suppression."[36] In the next chapter we look at emerging trends that could make the piracy problem more threatening or possibly better managed in the future. We conclude Chapter 7 with avenues to consider for resolving gaps in the short and long term.

7 Emerging trends and future directions

- **Emerging trends**
- **Long-term solutions: identifying stable and systemic solutions to piracy**
- **Conclusion**

While the fundamental act of piracy is largely the same as it has been throughout history, the technological, legal, and moral context that it takes place in has shifted dramatically. An important codicil to this is that while piracy as an act remains fundamentally the same as it was in the past, the specific tactics and elements that define modern piracy change as pirates and those working to counter piracy develop new approaches. In this chapter we examine new and developing trends in piracy, particularly how Somali piracy has become more violent and how the navies, shippers, and flag states have recalculated their responses to piracy based on this increasing violence. We next discuss what the long-term solution to piracy may look like. As discussed throughout the book piracy results from a failure of governance on the local, regional, and global level and efforts to fill gaps in the system can work either within or across each of these levels.

We do not offer a definitive solution to piracy: piracy has developed to its current levels in part because the competing needs of the various actors (for security, profit, sovereignty, or other desires) have made it difficult to identify a solution which is universally accepted. Because of this, there are real political and practical drawbacks to almost any solution to piracy. This may not always be the case: the changing face of modern piracy, and the growing international recognition that it is a serious problem requiring a serious attempt at solution, mean that the political and practical stumbling blocks to each potential solution may not be a constant. As the impact of piracy changes, the cost-to-benefit calculation correspondingly changes, and previously undesirable approaches may be seen as more reasonable. In this chapter, therefore, we use the previous analysis of the problems and gaps which facilitate piracy to suggest some pathways forward that may be useful directions for counterpiracy, while acknowledging the current challenges that make each approach difficult to put into practice.

The potential solutions start with coastal states: if coastal states are the primary lines of defense, then they must be considered as potential paths to future suppression of piracy. Where this is not feasible, or as a backup to this approach, the capacities of flag states must be brought more into line with their historical responsibilities, or their historical responsibilities must be transferred to more capable parties. Finally, as a safeguard to failures in these two systems, and as a way of resolving some of the competing desires among the various actors in piracy, global governance systems relating to piracy must be established, either jointly or separately by the private sector.

Emerging trends

One problem with the term piracy is that it implies uniformity, by lumping together the behavior of seaborne robbers in all corners of the world. This is, of course, not true, and as discussed earlier in the book the behavior and strategies of pirates throughout the world's pirate "hot spots" can vary dramatically. Alongside this implication of regional uniformity is also the problem of suggesting uniformity in behavior over time. This is not the case—piracy is not a static phenomenon, and neither are the strategies and tactics used by those who attempt to suppress pirates. As with almost any militarized conflict, the opposing actors involved in piracy and piracy suppression are actively engaged in a figurative (and possibly literal) arms race, with each group attempting to develop new approaches to meet their goals. Somali piracy and counterpiracy in particular have evolved dramatically since 2009. Specific trends include the geographic expansion of Somali pirates reach, an increase in the cost of ransoms and length of captivity, and what appears to be an increasing frequency of violence and abuse directed towards hostages. Some of the world's navies have responded to this with increased violence in their counterpiracy operations.[1]

One trend in Somali piracy that appears to have taken firm root is the development of "mother ships." Previous to this development Somali pirates, using primarily small skiffs, had a limited operational area. In 2010, pirates increasingly began to use captured ships to store fuel and food to significantly extend their operational range.[2] These captured mother ships are used to resupply the small skiffs, which, because of their speed, are used as attack boats. The mother ships are also used to hold captives for use as human shields. The use of these mother ships has allowed pirates to expand their zone of activity from the previously expected danger zone in the Gulf of Aden to within 300 miles of the Indian mainland. This development followed an increase in operations close to Somali shores by EUNAVFOR in an attempt to interdict pirates as they headed out to sea, and it is possible that the development of mother ships was spurred by this increase in operations. The mother ships allowed the pirates to more easily avoid near-shore enforcement, and may have also significantly contributed to an increase in pirates' capacity to operate during the monsoon months.[3] It appears that this approach is becoming a standard operating tactic for the pirates, dramatically expanding the threat they pose.

The average cost of a ransom and the average length of negotiations appear to be increasing as well. Over the past several years, the average ransom for ships and crews has steadily climbed.[4] As a consequence of increasing negotiation time, hostages endure longer captivity, with the average hostage experience increasing from three months in 2008 to over five months in 2010. The increased time of these hostage experiences greatly increases the physical and psychological risks to seafarers, because while in captivity they lack access to clean drinking water, sufficient quantities of food, proper medical care, as well as experiencing the potential abuse from the pirates themselves.[5]

The threat posed by pirates on their hostages is real: the violence associated with piracy appears to be becoming both more frequent and more severe.[6] In a recent statement the commander of EUNAVFOR stated that pirates were using torture as a method to extract information from hostages or to force navies to reject rescue attempts.[7] This may be due to changes in the source and backgrounds of Somali pirates, as the fishers who made up the initial pirate and "coast guard" bands are increasingly displaced by hardened fighters drawn from the interior of Somalia and by the lure of the money available through piracy.

The increase in time, expense, and violence associated with hostage-taking, has been paralleled by an increasing willingness for militaries and private guards to use force against pirates. In May 2011 the Indonesian navy became the first known navy to kill pirates in (what was reported as) an otherwise non-combat situation in which the pirates were not firing at the navy.[8]

Alongside this trend by uniformed military forces, violence from private armed guards is becoming more common. As of March 2011, an increasing number of maritime security professionals and even seafarer associations have begun to call for the placement of armed guards on ships. Citing rising brutality, the secretary-general of the International Chamber of Shipping Peter Hinchcliffe recommended "that the use of armed guards be permitted by the flag state when considered appropriate."[9] While the legality of this approach has not yet been settled, flag states do have the right to better define the legality of weapons on board their ships and the conditions for their use. A serious concern remains about ships carrying volatile cargos and the possibility of an increasing cycle of violence.

There is some potential support for this concern: the first known Somali pirate death from shipboard guards was in March 2010, where an armed security detail onboard the *MV Alemazaan* returned fire against a pirate attack.[10] The chronology of this specific attack suggests that pirates are willing to engage with armed guards: although the pirates initially withdrew when fired upon, they regrouped and made a second attack, which resulted in a sustained gunfight.

In all, the history of Somali piracy since 2009 has shown a steady increase in the money associated with attacks, in the operational sophistication and range of the pirates themselves, and in the willingness of pirates and counterpiracy operations to use violence. These trends are clearly dangerous: they demonstrate a continuing escalation of the economic, physical, and likely the psychological costs associated with piracy for all the related actors. If these trends continue, the pressure on counterpiracy groups to engage in more significant or costly efforts may be significant. The next section examines what some of these long-term solutions may be.

Long-term solutions: identifying stable and systemic solutions to piracy

The current responses to piracy and emerging trends in counterpiracy operations described throughout the book share a key characteristic—all of the identified responses, whether military, regional, institutional, or industrial, are fundamentally attempts to create limited and localized responses that address some symptoms of the piracy problem. However, as discussed in Chapter 6, this limited approach does not address the fundamental problems that allow piracy to flourish. The threat of piracy is a global phenomena. Actual piracy can occur at any time, or place, that an internationally recognized government fails to exercise effective and responsible control over its coastline. Its impact can be felt first at the local level, but eventually at the regional and then global. While it is crucial to resolve problems in a single state, such as Somalia, it is equally vital to address the global problem of piracy when a state, for whatever reason, fails to adequately supress piracy from its shore. Today the tools available to deal with the failure of a sovereign state to meet its obligations to other states, and the international community as a whole, are very blunt, expensive, and unattractive. As in the past it is largely a military response. More attractive solutions necessarily require rethinking a wider governance approach than is used by the current system.

History demonstrates that on-shore issues are critical to the prevention of piracy, and suppression activities have often involved on-shore elements designed to change the economic and personal risk-to-benefit ratio associated with piracy. An ideal solution to modern piracy would be one that developed or supported coastal states in the establishment of stable governance systems that could act as a deterrent against pirates operating in the region. Realistically, there are enormous challenges associated with this. Piracy thrives in failed states or other areas where significant governance systems have collapsed or are particularly weak.

The creation of more effective government by local elements is uncertain and may be both time consuming and violent. The creation or imposition of effective governance by foreign powers is difficult and requires a substantial political and economic commitment. History teaches us that such a commitment is only likely to be forthcoming from maritime powers closely linked to their merchant fleets.

While the obvious lesson seems to be that future policy needs to encourage the flag states to gain more capacity, or to encourage merchant fleets to register in states with more capacity to protect them, the actual lesson is not that clear. Flag state responsibility operated within the traditional international relations system, in which war and occupation of foreign lands were common activities. Suppressing piracy was often an opportunity for powerful states to exert political control over weaker states. Reversion to this model could be described as a return to a military model. Wide recognition of human rights, and particularly the right of self-determination, weakens the appeal of this model in the modern world.

If flag states' cannot, will not, or should not exercise their treaty-based responsibilities as the second line of defense, history is silent as to what institutions or structures could acquire such responsibility and exercise them effectively. For over a century, the European empires created institutions, such as the admiralty courts, that provided effective prosecution and deterrence of piracy with less military force than was exerted earlier. By developing institutions that meet the needs of both the states and the maritime industry, this institutional model has the potential of finding a less violent solution to the scourge of piracy. It is here that a more flexible approach to governance may bear the most fruit.

When coastal states and the flag states fail to provide adequate defense, the last line of defense against piracy has traditionally been self-defense by the merchant ships as represented by the Hanseatic League or the various East India Companies of European origin. This approach can be described as privatizing the solution. Privatized models tend to emphasize avoidance and defense over capture and prosecution, and create high levels of vulnerability to those merchants inevitably left out of the system. These three models are not exclusive, and the best solutions are likely to come out of a creative combination of features found in the different models.

Actors for whom piracy is of significant importance will need to work together to develop new structures of governance which work to fill these existing gaps.

The above analysis suggests what characteristics are necessary for the long-term suppression of piracy: a multi-level solution which includes support for coastal states, changes to the flag system, and a global structure which could respond to failures of the first two levels. Specific policy recommendations, however, are difficult to extract from this as each potential practical implementation of these characteristics faces significant pushback from stakeholders and other challenges associated with the political, economic, and social pressures that act on modern institutions. Although we do not offer specific recommendations we do lay out directions that could be pursued for developing systemic, long-term solutions to piracy on-shore, through the flagging system, or through broader governance structures. In the end the decisions will need to be made by the various stakeholders collectively.

Coastal states: on-shore economic and political development

If coastal states are the primary defense against piracy, then it is reasonable to look for solutions to piracy by focusing on coastal states. This is problematic: as discussed throughout the book, piracy appears where coastal states have failed. In the case of Somalia, attempts to revitalize onshore government have consistently failed. Despite the lack of an international mandate for regional states to become involved, a major focus of the UNODC and the Contact Group's Working Group 2 has been on developing the legal and enforcement institutions in the region around Somalia to improve the ability of courts in the region to hold and try pirates. The focus of the UNODC is on improving the legal system in Somalia itself.[11] The intractable governance problems that have contributed to the long-term chaos in Somalia make this challenging. As a result, the current programs have focused on supporting the expansion of prison and court capacity in regional neighbors including Kenya and the Seychelles. However, the capacity of both countries remains extremely small. Economic development activities in Somalia have included a focus on the creation of alternative economic activities and governance institutions. Both in the form of engagement with the TFG and the "dual-track" strategy of engagement with the Puntland government in partnership with the TFG, onshore development in Somalia has not yielded significant fruit. However, there is still the potential that the development of governance or economic activities in coastal states could play a significant role in the suppression of piracy.

One approach would be to focus primarily on the economic aspect of piracy. Piracy scholar Martin Murphy and developmental expert, Joseph Saba have laid out a variety of novel suggestions for economic development in Somalia.[12] They argue that as piracy is fundamentally an economic crime, alternative economic activities are a key factor in shifting the risk-to-reward ratio essential for a humane and sustainable solution to piracy. They call for a variety of development approaches, including the development of Somali ports, the reinvigoration of animal-based agriculture, and the exploitation of natural resources including mineral wealth and fishing. This is similar to the "constructive disengagement" approach championed by Bronwyn Bruton,[13] which calls for engagement with the Somali expatriate community to build the economy of Somalia while stepping back international aid and other forms of engagement. Both of these approaches argue that the collapse of the Somali economy underpins the continuing lack of governance on-shore, and that solutions to piracy must necessarily start by encouraging alternate forms of economic activity. The assumption is that stable governance can grow out of a stable Somali economy, funded by taxes and fees.

There are significant challenges with the implementation of these development programs, and serious concerns that in the absence of more targeted anti-piracy operations the first impact of an improved Somali economy will be more money available for outfitting pirate crews. Moreover, the instability and lack of governance in Somalia is a major, potentially fatal, flaw in any attempts to develop the Somali economy. These plans do have a unique benefit—rather than simply increasing the costs of piracy through military or legal suppression of piracy, these approaches provide alternate jobs that may draw potential pirates away from piracy.

However, the assumptions behind such an approach are subject to challenge. The residents of Somaliland, approximately the northern third of Somalia, declared independence in 1991 and instituted a government structure that effectively suppresses piracy in their territory. Somiland was not much richer than other parts of Somalia, and at the time it declared independence, it had poorer educational opportunities. It had no universities. Yet poverty does not compel its youth to seek a fortune through piracy.

A good case can be made that rewarding good governance, by providing development assistance to well governed areas, might be a stronger policy than rewarding bad governance by providing aid to pirate havens. However, Somaliland's government has gone unrecognized by any state.

In a much broader context, what states have not been willing to do, is question the assumptions that underlie international recognition of weak or failed states—states that fail to represent all their residents. Somaliland indicates that the United Nations respect for Somalia's sovereignty and territorial integrity exceeds that of many Somalis. History shows that sovereigns who could not, or would not, exercise control over a portion of their territory found other sovereigns annexing or encroaching on the territory. This had a tendency to eliminate weak sovereigns and the problems caused by them. On the negative side, European states found most non-European sovereigns relatively weak and built vast colonial empires by annexing their territory. Over the last 60 years, these empires have largely been dismantled; in large part based on acceptance of the principle of self-determination. Yet the idea of self-determination has not helped Somaliland gain acceptance at the international level.

In general, an approach that emphasizes local governance is probably a critical part of the long-term solution to piracy. The enormous challenges associated with re-establishing a failed state in general (much less the specific challenges found in Somalia) make this recommendation somewhat facetious. While coastal governance is critical for the long-term suppression of piracy, the actual on-the-ground facts of any specific failed state may make it impossible to create in any reasonable time—at least in time to provide relief to mariners. If the solution to piracy cannot be found in bolstering coastal state governance, then the solution must be found in other areas.

Even if a solution can be found in creating a functioning government, it is not a sufficient response. It is a very location specific solution that could lead to the international community lurching from one pirate hotspot to another, as indicated by UN Security Council Resolution 2018 (2011) starting afresh with condemning piracy in West

Africa.[14] Focusing development resources on piracy centers could even encourage poor countries to engage in piracy to attract international development attention.

Empowering flag states

If involvement with the coastal state does not offer a near-term solution, then historically the flag states have assumed an obligation to protect their ships. However, the flag states of the twenty-first century do not have the naval capacity to engage pirates hundreds or even thousands of miles away, nor the political and economic resources required to build such a capacity. Nevertheless, that does not mean the flag states are powerless or should be ignored. The formal power of the flag state is significant. For example, they can determine what weapons can be carried aboard ships registered in their state, and set standards for their use. They can investigate and prosecute crimes committed aboard their flagged vessels. They can determine if they will require safe-rooms, and how those rooms are to be constructed. In general, they do few of these things because they lack the incentive and resources. If the formal powers of the flag state can be augmented in non-traditional ways, and incentives provided that make them want to accept more responsibility, the modern flag states could have a significant impact.

That is the idea behind the proposal of Jardine Lloyd Thompson Group, a London insurance firm that insures 14 percent of the world's commercial shipping fleet. They propose a private navy for anti-piracy operation around Somalia. Fast patrol boats with armed guards would provide a Convoy Escort Program for maritime traffic through the danger zone. It would be constituted as a naval auxiliary to a flag state. It would be funded by the maritime industry through insurance premiums or savings in the premium being directed to a non-profit naval corporation. In theory, the flag state would be using its sovereign right to deploy a navy to engage pirates, a right no private company has under UNCLOS. However, the costs will be entirely born by others. The sponsors claim a flag state is interested in the proposal.[15]

The associated legal challenge has, however, not yet been resolved. Recalling from Chapter 1 that privateers were considered naval auxiliaries in the past, it is not clear how this structure would be materially or legally different, and it would certainly face many traditional problems associated with wartime convoys including increasing the danger to those who drop out of a convoy due to mechanical or other problems.

Another approach to building flag state capacity would be the empowerment of crewmembers or private guards with official status in the flag state. This would be similar to a bill passed in the United States post-9/11 that gave cockpit crew the right (but not the obligation) to carry arms to defend the cockpit. The crew pays for their own training and weapons and are designated as Deputy US Air Marshalls. If they use lethal force to protect their cockpit they carry the same immunities to prosecution as federal government law enforcement employees operating in the line of duty. If a flag state were to offer a similar program for crew members and commercial guards on their flagged ship, it could clear up some of the legal liabilities of arming ships by establishing clear rules of engagement and legal mandates for the use of force. A sea marshall program could be run without net cost to the flag states with support from insurance companies, industry, and other states if such funding were able to be identified. Such a system would work with the existing norms rather than against them, but has not been subject to serious consideration. Operational details including the source and structure of funding need more significant development if this plan is considered.

An alternate pathway for flag states to protect ships is through support for the placement of armed guards onboard vessels. Initial steps on this approach have been taken by the Marshall Islands registry in its support for the Security Association for the Maritime Industry (SAMI). SAMI is an association founded in 2011 with the goal of developing standards for the use of private security guards, along with vetting criteria to ensure that private guards are appropriately trained and professional.[16] By supporting SAMI, the Marshall Islands are exploring one way that flag states can support ships' defense without the development of additional naval capacities or increased costs. This is a move to privatizing piracy defense. All of these plans suffer from focusing only on ship protection rather than a balance between protection and criminal prosecution.

Flag states might also take on a role of providing a legitimate venue for piracy prosecution. UNCLOS and common law gives flag states special standing to enforce criminal laws against crimes that occur aboard their ships. While prosecution and incarceration can be costly, flag states might offer registered ship-owners insurance policies guaranteeing them a venue for prosecution if pirates are captured attacking their ship. Since the incidents of piracy are only a small percentage of all shipping, flag states might gain revenue and a favorable reputation for developing institutions that help in the management of piracy.

In all, there are several approaches that can be taken to build flag state capacity to defend ships flagged in their country. Each of these approaches faces potential practical and political challenges, reflecting the complexity of the legal and operational questions posed by piracy, but they also face the benefit of being relatively small adjustments to the current international registry system. If these challenges prove to be too significant, and these approaches do not gain traction, a more radical re-evaluation of the system may be required.

Moving beyond flag states

An alternate approach to dealing with the role of flag states is to create systems that move beyond the traditional conceptions of the flag state by developing new structures or approaches to ship registration. This is not necessarily a novel concept—the development of the International Convention for the Prevention of Pollution from Ships was in response to poor open-registry compliance to environmental inspections. Although ship owners and flag states were not absolved of their responsibilities, port states receiving cargo from ships of a foreign flag were given inspection rights and a right to detain foreign ships until repairs or compliance was achieved. A similar model could allow port states to impose minimum piracy suppression standards on ships that call at their ports, or employ crewmembers from their state. A few key states such as the United States, EU member states, and Japan could threaten to impose such rules unilaterally, bringing the issues to the forefront of international discussions.

Already under discussion is the development of an international ship protection force. Rather than each flag state providing armed guards to protect their ships, or private companies providing armed guards under contract to ship-owners, "blue helmets", or soldiers assigned to the United Nations could take on the role. These guards would have the same immunities from prosecution as flag state soldiers and could provide less exclusionary coverage. This could be made even more radical, by a movement to create an international registry under the UN, which would then assume the traditional flag state role of providing piracy protection and prosecutions. Such a registry could be as an alternative to the flag state system or a replacement of it.

This global registry could assume the responsibility for implementation and enforcement of maritime standards and criminal investigation and prosecution on the high seas, in much the same way that traditional flag states acted. The funding for such a registry could be obtained through the fees associated with registration. Panama is reported to earn about $20 million from its registry with 22 percent of the world's dead weight tons.[17] If revenue is proportional to tonnage then around $90 million is collected globally for ship registration. This is more than twice the

2011 budget of the IMO. A specialized global register that devotes all of the registration revenue to maritime regulation and enforcement might be a substantial improvement over the current dispersed system. To push this idea even further, if recognized as an international regulator having the equivalent of a sovereign's control over ships, a global registry could undertake enforcement actions, arbitration, and admiralty court operations including a criminal court and prison facilities to try and incarcerate pirates. Aside from the legal questions associated with such potential activities, such a monopoly registration system would face much resistance from the shipping industry, which currently benefits from the ability to "shop around" to identify flag states with favorable regulations. Significant pushback from shippers could be expected from any attempts to move in the direction of a global registry, unless the potential benefits of such a move were clearly elucidated and presented.

If these challenges prove too significant, or if political and contextual pressures push the solution of piracy away from both coastal states and engagement with the flag system, the solution to piracy will need to be found in a novel, systemic approach. Some strategy which improves the capacity of the multiplicity of actors working to suppress piracy will need to be developed. This could include a focus on the international military response, legal or jurisdictional issues, business, or a multi-actor, comprehensive approach.

Improving the international military response through changing capacities or coordination

One potential option for a systematic solution to piracy not found in the coastal or flag states is to improve the capacity of the naval forces operating to counter piracy. As discussed in Chapter 6, the current military response off Somalia is a hodgepodge of three international groups, with distinct missions and mandates. The EUNAVFOR, NATO, and multinational CTF-151 missions each have their own organizational and operational structures, with independent missions. This raises significant problems of redundancy and inefficiency in force distribution and causes challenges for information sharing. The international military forces have attempted to resolve some of these problems through the SHADE initiative, which provides a structure for information sharing and the reduction of conflicts between the different organizations that operate in the region. This does not address some core problems with the current patchwork structure.

One of these problems is that national groups, and even regional groups made up of a limited group of states, inevitably prioritize their national interests. When US interests demanded a naval presence near Libya, ships were removed from counterpiracy operations,[18] and protection operations in international waters offer many chances for navies to prioritize protecting their own national ships over the most efficient or best overall protective process.

A second core problem with the current system is that because the major international forces are deployed through existing treaty bodies such as the EU or NATO, countries which are external to these bodies do not have an opportunity to participate in coordinated counterpiracy actions without subordinating themselves into a chain of command they have no voice in.

A multinational, coordinated structure that subsumed all the existing naval missions into one coordinated command and left the door open for participation by new naval forces could significantly improve the efficient coordination of information and assets among all the different naval forces operating in the region. An appealing way of creating this structure would be through the UN, which may have the legal authority to develop a coordinated naval force in the region. If such a force were developed with a clear mandate, it is possibly that there would be significant improvements in coordination and efficiency, and a significant reduction in administrative costs.

Such a coordinated multinational response has all the problems of any military-based solution, including the lack of adequate naval resources overall. While some may see it as a significant improvement in operational terms over the current structure, there are practical problems that pose stumbling blocks to the implementation of this approach. Ideally, it serves as a model for the effective response to piracy outside of Somalia and other problems of violent conflict in global commons, by demonstrating how higher levels of coordination than that which is available at the national or regional levels can give significant improvements over responses based at these lower levels. However, such a step would require Security Council action, and it is unlikely that several of the permanent members would agree to such a system. It would also suffer, as other security council peacekeeping missions do, in that placing military forces under UN command is entirely a voluntary contribution by each participating country, which may limit the resources devoted to it.

A second potential option for increasing military effectiveness, without more violence on land would be to address the disconnect between the military and legal mission. Currently, many navies do not have legal training in rules of evidence or significant capacity to function effectively in a law enforcement role. This could be addressed by reinstituting the concepts of admiralty courts or military commissions to quickly provide a more robust prosecutorial venue for captured pirates. The navies of the world have effectively abandoned the historical precedents of judging pirates in Admiralty, Vice Admiralty courts, or other forms of special colonial commissions. These courts played an important role in suppressing piracy from the 1700s through to about the mid-twentieth century. One advantage of these courts was that they did not depend on other sovereign states for their formation or legitimacy. Another is that they could be formed quickly all over the world, even aboard ships. In theory a piracy court to deal with East African piracy could be established in Diego Garcia, a British territory in the middle of the Indian Ocean by resurrecting their admiralty courts. The French could also establish such courts in their overseas department of Reunion.

Such action would likely be within the guidelines of Article 105 of UNCLOS which states "The courts of the State which carried out the seizure may decide upon the penalties to be imposed ..." This may address several current problems with the prosecution of piracy. With merchant crews and naval force likely coming from several countries, it is difficult and expensive to ensure the availability of live witnesses in a distant court months after a pirate attack. The ability of admiralty courts or military commissions to establish rules of evidence that would permit written, videotaped or even remote video testimony could be important in seeing the judicial process through. In addition the rapidity and flexible location for such a court can meet the requirements for judicial deterrence mentioned in Chapter 5 of speedy and certain justice process. Such courts might even reduce the burden of the court in bringing in witnesses. They may already be there, still serving on the naval ship involved.

Practically, this would have significant challenges. This proposal is unlikely to receive a broad international mandate if one state were to attempt to form such a commission, particularly if it was the United States. If any of the great powers tried to establish a military commission it would almost certainly entail new national legislation and would be portrayed in much of the world as a return to colonial justice. Criticism of this idea was perhaps best summed up by the German Defense Minister Franz Josef Jung who said that a piracy court " ... needs to be an international authority. No one wants a 'Guantanamo on the sea.'"[19] If several states joined together to form such a commission or to allow multiple commissions it might be more politically acceptable, but the legal complexity would multiply. Practically, it may be hard to find a military power, even a regional military power, that would have both the credibility and desire to form such a commission.

Collective cooperation and the shipping industry

Another systemic approach to reducing piracy is found not with the military response, but with the shipping industry. The role of the shipping industry in responding to piracy has been complicated by divisions and a lack of coordination both within the industry and between the industry and other sectors. Within the industry, there is the significant problem that compliance with BMP is essentially a decision made by shipowners on a ship-by-ship basis. Although BMP appears successful in reducing the danger to ships, industry compliance with BMP is currently inconsistent. In a recent speech, IMO Secretary-General Efthimios Mitropoulos reported compliance rates of only 40 percent, and some estimates place the number as low as 20 percent.[20] There is no collective, internal system by which compliance with BMP is either mandated or tracked. How much this contributes directly to the slow and uneven adoption of BMP on ships, even though these practices appear to significantly reduce the numbers of successful attacks cannot be known without tracking information Analysis of non-compliant ships may reveal that the ships lack a capacity to comply, or that they are engaged in other illegal activities such as human trafficking, arms trade, dumping, smuggling, poaching fish, or drug trade.

Some form of collective coordination among industry players may be necessary to increase compliance with BMP if the preceding factors are not significant. As discussed above, suggestions along this line have tended to emphasize mandates by flag states, although enforcement of such mandates is still an issue. Other approaches include a "name and shame" approach that uses soft pressure to encourage ships to comply or a harder approach from the insurance industry that requires ships to use BMP in order to retain insurance coverage in the affected areas. Some form of internal, collective coordination among all levels of the industry which encourages seafarers, shipowners, and shipping companies to work together to mandate BMP, may prove to be an effective tool particularly if it adjusts BMP to be applicable in more situations.

There is also the problem of coordination between industry and other sectors. Although industry has a critical interest in the piracy, there have been few attempts to bring it into the decision-making structure of groups formed to combat piracy. While the international contact groups have asked industry to donate to trust funds, there has not been a serious attempt to bring industry into the decision-making process. Without closing this gap, it is hard to imagine industry becoming fully invested in any attempt to resolve piracy that is executed by transnational bodies.

A global framework for pirate governance

All of the above proposed solutions, while representing approaches to deal with piracy from the viewpoint of improving governance around the issue, share a fundamental problem: they each approach the problem of piracy from a limited and specific perspective, whether that of states, the military, or industry. The reality of piracy is that it affects all these sectors, and is rooted in problems arising in domains outside of these sectors. It is unlikely that any plan or approach will prove to be a silver bullet that suppresses piracy. Instead, the complicated and multifaceted problems that lead to the development of piracy will require a multifaceted, coordinated response. Moreover, as discussed above each proposed approach faces potential pushback or resistance from stakeholders or other groups associated with piracy. Any solution proposed to address piracy that comes from one sector is likely to face problems in moving to implementation, unless the concerns of all the actors affected by the solution are accommodated in some way. This suggests that some form of coordinated engagement among all of the stakeholders associated with the problem of piracy—including industry, flag states, the military, coastal states, seafarer associations, and others—is likely to represent the best approach to developing a solution to piracy. A working group, association, or other decision-making structure that brought together these stakeholders would have the capacity to develop a multi-step, coordinated, and comprehensive approach to the issue of piracy, and also allow stakeholders to represent their specific needs and concerns in a structure that would allow for the development of a collective decision or compromise endorsed by all actors. This approach represents possibly the only truly effective strategy that would allow piracy to be addressed in a comprehensive and effective way.

This kind of multi-stakeholder coordinated response, while clearly of critical importance, is a difficult system to develop. Many transnational decision-making bodies focus exclusively on one sector (most often the state, as in the case of the UN) and explicitly exclude other sectors from participation in the decision-making structure. Governance structures are needed which are responsive and inclusive of all the affected groups, and which have both the authority and the capacity to develop and execute plans to solve critical problems like piracy. In the case of piracy the existing groups and coordinating bodies do not meet this criterion.

One project working in this direction is the Oceans Beyond Piracy (OBP) project.[21] This is a multiyear process which brings together key actors in all of the sectors affected by piracy to develop a multi-sector coordinated plan to address piracy. As of spring 2011, this project has established a working group dedicated to the collective resolution of piracy. While it is too early to tell what solutions this group may develop, some ideas could include movements to standardize national piracy codes, support regional law enforcement development, expand the industry BMP to increase compliance, and integrate the perspectives of industry and other actors into the decision and implementation of plans of action developed by national and regional groups. The core goal of the OBP project is to develop a new type of governance, driven less by the current legal frameworks of institutions and states and more by a practical approach to problem-solving driven by the critical need for a solution to piracy as a pressing transnational problem that may require amending the current allocations of responsibility or improve the capacity of responsible parties to respond.

The OBP project represents one of the few attempts to develop an inclusive and legitimate multi-stakeholder process for resolving piracy. Regardless of the success or failure of this specific initiative, piracy is ultimately facilitated by failures and inadequacies of governance structures at almost all levels; from the states which allow safe havens to form, to states that allow predation of ships flagged in their names, to the shipowners and industries which choose not to follow existing BMP, to the transnational bodies attempting to commit sufficient military and judicial resources to the enforcement of antipiracy laws. Because of this fact, the ultimate solution to piracy is not likely to come from any one sector: it will require a significant and coordinated action among many different sectors to create a shared governance structure.

Conclusion

Piracy presents an intriguing problem. Human societies have dealt with piracy for all of recorded human history. The act of piracy has not changed: pirates try to create a local advantage, and hit the strong where they are weak. This has been upon the sea, far from the victim's home, and far from any assistance. To corrupt an old Chinese saying, "The oceans are wide and the Emperor is far away."

Given this history, one would hope that humanity would have learned to effectively suppress piracy. In certain ways it has. It has resolved severe outbreaks of piracy through war and occupation, through criminalization and the prosecution, conviction and execution (or incarceration) of pirates, and through the expectations that merchant ships would defend themselves. As this book demonstrates, for a variety of sometimes very good reasons many of these responses are not available today.

Society let the institutions of the nineteenth and early twentieth century, which had successfully criminalized piracy, be dismantled. It did so because of changing international norms, and the recognition of the intrinsic human rights of the individual. International custom and the United Nation's Charter now endorses self-determination—the right of individuals to live in a community of their own choosing. As a result, dismantling the great European empires of the nineteenth and twentieth centuries became a powerful international focus over the last 60 years. The empires were dismantled along with their globe spanning judicial institutions that had been used to criminalize and suppress piracy. It is not a coincidence that the British decision to pull back its naval presence "East of the Suez" in 1971 coincides with increasing piracy.

We no longer consider the acts of pirates to be an indictment of the entire community in which they live. We accept the individual's intrinsic human rights and the individual's intrinsic human responsibility for their own behavior. Piracy is no longer *casus bellum*. In itself it is not terrorism. It is a crime of an individual and the group of individuals who directly support that crime—the accomplices, piratical companions, and, if they exist, the criminal bosses and financiers. But it is also a crime which society no longer has the institutions of justice to control.

For most of history, the trade of a country was carried by its merchants on ships flying the flag of their country. Rulers identified with their ships. As is true with naval ships today, the ships of a country projected its power and prestige wherever they went. By custom, the laws of the state and even its territory extended onto the ships that flew its flag. An attack on a ship was an attack on the nation. If a man preyed upon his own community, it was a heinous crime on par with treason. If the pirate was from another community, sovereigns responded to such piracy, when they wanted to, as a war with the pirate community and its sovereign. Protecting one's merchant fleet was a matter of national honor. There was often little distinction made between those who went out in ships as pirates and those who stayed at home as demonstrated by the brutal bombardment of Algeria in 1815. All shared the collective guilt of being from a pirate community.

Much has changed in the maritime world. In the last half of the twentieth century, European empires were dismantled and more than 100 new sovereign countries were created. This not only created a high potential for weak states, where pirates could find safe haven, it also eliminated the colonial judicial institutions such as the English Vice Admiralty Courts. However, by nearly 200 years of colonial custom, piracy had become a crime and that designation was enshrined in UNCLOS in 1982 and in the 1958 treaty that preceded it. Not much thought was given to the importance of the imperial legal institutions in making criminalization work or the implications of their decline.

At the same time, the shipping industry started to flee from belligerent states, that included all of the naval powers, to open registry states. They stayed because they realized lower operational costs. From 2 percent in 1947 to 55 percent of commercial tonnage in 2011[22] became registered in the open registries of small states. Such a massive flight from the maritime powers was facilitated by the belief that piracy was no longer a serious threat. This reflagging fundamentally changed and reduced the political accountability and responsiveness of the maritime powers to the merchant fleet. By both customary and international convention the safety of a vessel was the responsibility of the owners and ensured by the state whose flag the ship flew. These customs and laws were created largely before the impact of open registries was fully appreciated. The new flag states retained the traditional flag state responsibilities but were often both incapable and unwilling to assume them.

In addition, the volume of world trade has grown almost 30 times since 1950 and transportation costs have fallen by 70 percent. This has greatly increased the number of ships, with the registered fleet growing five times since 1950 to nearly 100,000 ships, about half of which carry freight in international commerce. Technology has developed sophisticated control and cargo handling systems. Growth provides more targets for pirates, and the drop in costs and technology mean that larger ships are sailing with smaller crews making them more vulnerable.

What has occurred has been an extraordinary convergence of seemingly unrelated trends that collectively created an environment where piracy can flourish on the ground and water, yet the responsibility to respond has been diffused. The proximate cause of piracy is the failure of both coastal state and the open registry flag states to live up to their international responsibilities. In both cases caused by a shift of those responsibilities from powerful states to weak states.

This was coupled with changes in the maritime industry structures and technology that were not reflected by corresponding changes in customs, regulations, and institutions.

The global response can have elements from only three models. Pirates could face increased military action. Meeting violence with violence is a traditional response, but is very location specific and resource intensive. The current futility of military patrols, hamstrung by judicially inspired rules of engagement, but a lack of judicial capacity and institutions to handle detainees, is leading to both mission fatigue and a push, by some, for rules of engagement that are more combative. But military operations are difficult to maintain for extendended periods because the current posture is unsustainable. For promoting rule of law in global governance and for the protection of human rights, more combative military operations are an unattractive option. Unfortunately, this scenario becomes increasingly likely as the violence of piracy increases.

The second option is that merchant ships and mariners could take a more direct responsibility for the protection of their industry. This privatization of maritime security has historical precedence when states were unable or unwilling to provide security. Armed private guards, private convoy systems with armed escorts, mandated operating practices, changes in ship design and equipment, and other industry-funded activities are a viable but costly, risky, and stressful alternative to a faltering international response. Private protection tends to focus only on avoidance of successful hijacking, and may merely change the targets of pirates to unarmed or lightly armed ships. This option becomes increasingly likely as modern states fail to meet their traditional obligations to the industry and to each other.

The third option is to develop institutions that will be able to respond to outbreaks of piracy with more efficiency and effectiveness than either the military model or the private industry models alone. State responses would include more than a military response, and be coordinated with industry partners. A great deal of effort is being expended to create such institutions, but much of this effort has been uncoordinated, impractical, and unsustainable. It has had little real impact. Some efforts, such as the major focus on making regional states responsible for adjudicating the piratical activities of neighbouring states, are not supported by maritime tradition, international treaty obligations, or even a reasonable expectation that they can develop the capacity needed for an effective response.

Despite the plethora of civil, national, regional, and international organization discussed in Chapter 3, there is no single, responsible organization focused on developing and coordinating a comprehensive anti-piracy response. Behind all the furious and expensive efforts to suppress piracy, there is no strategic plan and no shared vision of how to protect maritime transport from piracy. More importantly, there is no governance structure that includes all the stakeholders with the responsibility of developing a feasible and comprehensive strategy. As a result, the responses—militarily, institutionally, and privately—have been, and continue to be haphazard, tactical, costly, and mostly ineffective. The recognition that nineteenth century rules and twentieth century institutions are not up to the task of suppressing piracy given twenty-first century social expectations, industry structure, and technology is a good place to start in the search for a modern governance solution to the persistent problem of maritime piracy.

Despite good intentions, the best we have to offer today is not enough.

Notes

Introduction

1 Kaija Hurlburt Eamon Aloyo, Jon Huggins, Jens V. Madsen, Kasey Pennington, Maisie Pigeon, and D. Conor Seyle, *The Human Cost of Somali Piracy*, Oceans Beyond Piracy, http://oceansbeyondpiracy.org/sites/default/files/human_cost_of_somali_piracy.pdf.

2 J. Peter Pham, *West African Piracy: Symptoms, Causes, and Responses*, briefing paper for the Global Challenge, Regional Responses: Forging a Common Approach to Maritime Piracy conference, April 2011, Dubai, United Arab Emirates, 30; and ICC International Maritime Bureau, "Piracy and Armed Robbery Against Ships," report for the period of 1 January–31 September 2010.

3 The costs can be broken down as follows: multinational naval coalitions—approximately $2 billion, judicial response—approximately $31 million, and combined budgets of counterpiracy organizations such as the International Maritime Organization—approximately $24.5 million.

1 Piracy: the nature of the problem

1 Edwin D. Dickenson, "Is the Crime of Piracy Obsolete?" *Harvard Law Review* Vol. 38, No. 3 (1925): 334.

2 Anna Bowden, "The Economic Cost of Maritime Piracy," One Earth Future, December 2010, http://oceansbeyondpiracy.org/documents/The_Economic_Cost_of_Piracy_Full_Report.pdf.

3 ICC International Maritime Bureau, "Piracy and Armed Robbery against Ships: Report for the Period of 1 January–31 March 2011" (London: ICC International Maritime Bureau, 2011).

4 Peter Lehr, *Violence at Sea: Piracy in the Age of Global Terrorism* (New York: Routledge, 2007), vii.

5 Adam J. Young, *Contemporary Maritime Piracy in Southeast Asia: History, Causes, Remedies* (Singapore: Institute of Southeast Asian Studies, 2007), 24–26.

6 Joshua Goodwin. "Universal Jurisdiction and the Pirate: Time for an Old Couple to Part," *Vanderbilt Journal of Transnational Law* 39, no. 3 (2006): 989.

7 Alfred P. Rubin, *The Law of Piracy* (Honolulu: University Press of the Pacific, 2006).

8 Noam Chomsky, *Pirates and Emperors, Old and New: International Terrorism in the Real World* (Brooklyn, NY: South End Press, 2003), vii.

9 *An Act for the Protection of the Commerce and Seamen of the United States, against the Tripolitan Cruisers*, chapter 4, 2 stat. 129, 130 (1802). "[I]t shall be lawful to equip, officer, man, and employ such of the armed vessels of the United States as may be judged requisite by the President ... for protecting effectually the commerce and seamen thereof on the Atlantic ocean, the Mediterranean and adjoining seas." Congress also authorized the president to issue orders to American public vessels "to subdue, seize and make prize of all vessels, goods and effects, belonging to the Bey of Tripoli, or to his subjects ... "

10 Angus Konstam, *Piracy: The Complete History* (Oxford: Osprey, 2008), 38.

11 *The Consulate of the Sea and Related Documents* (Stanley S. Jados, trans.), http://libro.uca.edu/consulate/consulate.htm.

12 John Steele Gordon, "Commerce Raider," *American Heritage* 46, no. 5 (1995).

13 Konstam, *Piracy: The Complete History*, 37.

14 *The Paris Declaration Respecting Maritime Law*, 16 April 1856, http://wwi.lib.byu.edu/index.php/Paris_Declaration_Respecting_Maritime_Law.

15 Lloyd's List, Controversial-Anti-Piracy-Plan-Revealed, http://www.lloydslistdcn.com.au/archive/2011/02-february/04/controversial-anti-piracy-plan-revealed.

16 Richard J. Goldstone and Adam M. Smith, *International Judicial Institutions: The Architecture of International Justice at Home and Abroad* (New York and Oxford: Routledge, 2009), 15.

17 Goldstone and Smith, *International Judicial Institutions*, 16.

18 Lawrence Azubuike, "International Law Regime against Piracy," *Annual Survey of International & Comparative Law* 15, no. 1 (2010). Available at: http://digitalcommons.law.ggu.edu/cgi/viewcontent.cgi?article=1127&context=annlsurvey.

19 United Nations Convention on the Law of the Sea, part VII.

20 United Nations Convention on the Law of the Sea.

21 Ibid.

22 Julian Ku, "Did the Israeli Defense Forces Commandos Commit 'Piracy'? Nope," http://opiniojuris.org/2010/06/01/did-the-israeli-defense-forces-commandos-commit-piracy-nope/.

23 Speech by Yoshiaki Ito, Executive Director of ReCAAP ISC, April 2007. See http://www.recaap.org/news/pdf/news/april07.pdf.

24 Martin N. Murphy, *Small Boats, Weak States, Dirty Money: Piracy and Maritime Terrorism in the Modern World* (New York: Columbia University Press, 2009), 8.

25 In2 East Africa, "L. Victoria Piracy Hinders EAC Common Market," 23 January 2011, http://in2eastafrica.net/l-victoria-piracy-hinders-eac-common-market.

26 Robbery ashore: US Code 18 U.S.C..81 § 1661.

27 Young, *Contemporary Maritime Piracy in Southeast Asia: History, Causes, Remedies*, 24–26.

28 Plutarch, "The Life of Pompey" in *The Parallel Lives*, Bernadotte Perrin, trans. (Cambridge, Mass.: Harvard University Press, 1917).

29 Martin N. Murphy, *Somalia: The New Barbary? Piracy and Islam in the Horn of Africa* (New York: Columbia University Press, 2011), 33.

30 Vijay Sakhuja, Sea Piracy in South Asia, http://www.saag.org/common/uploaded_files/paper1259.html.

31 James Kraska, "Freakonomics of Maritime Piracy," *Brown Journal of World Affairs* 16, no. 2 (2010): 116.

32 Stig Hansen, *Piracy in the Greater Gulf of Aden: Myths, Misconceptions and Remedies* (Oslo: Norwegian Institute for Urban and Regional Research, 2009).

33 With effect from 0001Z on 1 April 2011 the Extended Risk Zone is as follows: "The western border of the Zone runs from the coastline at the border of Djibouti and Somalia to position 11 48 N, 45 E; from 12 00 N, 45 E to Mayyun Island in the Bab El Mandeb Straits. The eastern border is set at 78 E, the southern border is set at 10 S and the Northern Border set at 26 N." Joint IBF Press Release, "International Bargaining Forum Reaches New Piracy Area Agreement," http://www.itfglobal.org/press-area/index.cfm/pressdetail/5818.

34 Roger Middleton, "Trends in Piracy: A Global Problem with Somalia at the Core," in *Global Challenge, Regional Responses: Forging a Common Approach to Maritime Piracy* (Dubai, UAE: Dubai School of Government, 2011), 23. Available at: http://counterpiracy.ae/briefing_papers/Middleton%20Trends%20in%20Piracy%20A%20Global%20Problem%20with%20Somalia%20at%20the%20Core.pdf.

35 Adam Corbett, "Double Edge to Relatively Quick Release of 'Irene SL,'" *TradeWinds*, 15 April 2011.

36 Middleton, "Trends in Piracy: A Global Problem with Somalia at the Core," 21.

37 J. Peter Pham, "West African Piracy: Symptoms, Causes, and Responses," in Global Challenge, Regional Responses: Forging a Common Approach to Maritime Piracy (Dubai, United Arab Emirates: Dubai School of Government, 2011), 30. Available at: http://counterpiracy.ae/briefing_papers/Pham%20West%20African%20Piracy%20-%20Symptoms%20Causes%20and%20Responses.pdf.

38 Ibid.

39 RiskIntelligence, Nigeria—Review of 2010 and Outlook for 2011, http://www.riskintelligence.eu/dyn/files/newspage_links/4-file/Nigeria%20Review%20of%202010%20and%20Outlook%20for%202011.pdf.

40 Young, *Contemporary Maritime Piracy in Southeast Asia: History, Causes, and Remedies*, 2.

41 John Roosa, "The Straits of Malacca: Gateway or Gauntlet?" *University of Toronto Quarterly* 74, no. 1 (2004/2005): 529.

42 Young, *Contemporary Maritime Piracy in Southeast Asia: History, Causes, and Remedies*, 2.

43 Simon Montlake, "Hard Times for Pirates in Busy World Waterway," *The Christian Science Monitor*, 30 October 2006.

44 Young, *Contemporary Maritime Piracy in Southeast Asia: History, Causes, and Remedies*, 2.

45 Kaija Hurlburt, "The Human Cost of Somali Piracy," One Earth Future, Oceans Beyond Piracy project, June 2011, http://oceansbeyondpiracy.org/sites/default/files/human_cost_of_somali_piracy.pdf. www.oceansbeyondpiracy.org.

46 Shipping companies and various government agencies keep data on hostage welfare based on interviews with seafarers post release. These data, however, are not shared with the public.

47 Hurlburt, "The Human Cost of Somali Piracy."
48 "Anti-Pirate Strategies Fail Beluga Nomination," Breakbulk, 3 February 2011. Available at: www.breakbulk.com/piracy/anti-pirate-strategies-fail-beluga-nomination
49 Hurlburt, "The Human Cost of Somali Piracy."
50 International Transport Workers' Federation, "Seafarer Boycott of Piracy Areas 'Now Possible,'" http://www.itfglobal.org/press-area/index.cfm/pressdetail/5705; and Lloyd's List, "Ransom Payments Escalate As Somali Pirates Up the Ante," http://www.lloydslist.com/ll/sector/ship-operations/article350209.ece.
51 Abukar Arman. Non-Military solutions to the Somali Piracy Dilemma, http://www.worldpress.org/Africa/3342.cfm.
52 Somalia Report, "Pirates Stealing Local Fishing Boats, Motors: Local Economy Devastated by Piracy in Bosaso," www.somaliareport.com/index.php/post/330.
53 Ibid.
54 Andrew Harding, "Postcard from Somali Pirate Capital," BBC, 16 June 2009. Available at: http://news.bbc.co.uk/2/hi/africa/8103585.stm.
55 Thanks to Anna Bowden for her research and writing in this section. For more information see "The Economic Cost of Piracy," One Earth Future, Oceans Beyond Piracy project.
56 Peter Lehr, ed., *Violence at Sea: Piracy in the Age of Global Terrorism* (New York: Routledge, 2007). This is a particularly low number since the shipping industry is in a recession. Typically the spot rate on a commercial vessel is at least $50,000 a day.
57 Datamonitor, "Global Marine Freight, Industry Profile, http://wenku.baidu.com/view/cc4eb66448d7c1c708a14529.html, 9. This is for total ocean going freight revenues.
58 Bowden, "The Economic Cost of Piracy."
59 See Ivan Dikov, "Seychelles Minister Joel Morgan: Somali Pirates Damage Both Maritime Trade and Regional Stability," Novinite (Sofia News Agency), 10 March 2010, www.novinite.com/view_news.php?id=114068; and Afrique Avenir, "Seychelles lost € 28 million in 2009 due to piracy, says minister," www.afriqueavenir.org/en/2010/04/07/seychelles-lost-e-28-million-in-2009-due-to-piracy-says-minister/.
60 Johnstone Ole Turana and Allan Odhiambo, "New piracy levy to push up the cost of imported goods," Business Daily, 9 March 2010, www.businessdailyafrica.com/Company%20Industry/New%20piracy%20levy%20to%20push%20up%20the%20cost%20of%20imported%20goods%20/-/539550/875618/-/149ru84/-/index.html; and Eric Van Der Linden, "Piracy: Why Kenya Should Care," AllAfrica.com, http://allafrica.com/stories/201004071011. html.
61 "Kenya loses out in cattle export deal over piracy," *Daily Nation*, 30 November 2011; and "Livestock Exports to Mauritius Threatened by Somali Pirates," *Daily Nation*, 2 January 2011.
62 Thanks to Eamon Aloyo for research on political costs of piracy.
63 Peter Chalk, RAND Project Air Force, "The Maritime Dimension of International Security: Terrorism, Piracy, and Challenges for the United States," http://www.rand.org/pubs/monographs/2008/RAND_MG697.pdf.
64 Peter Chalk, Rand Corporation, "Maritime Piracy, Reasons, Dangers, and Solutions," testimony presented before the House Transportation and Infrastructure Committee, Subcommittee on Coast Guard and Maritime

128   *Notes*

Transportation, 4 February 2009, http://www.dtic.mil/cgi-bin/GetTRDoc?
AD=ADA493656&Location=U2&doc=GetTRDoc.pdf.

65 Jeffrey Gettleman, "In Somali Civil War, Both Sides Embrace Pirates,"
New York Times, 1 September 2010, and "Ransoms and Hostages Increase
for Somali Pirates," *New York Times*, 9 November 2010.

66 Peter Pham, "Global Ripples from the Niger Delta," *Defense Review*
(2008). Available at http://worlddefensereview.com/pham071008.shtml.

67 Michael Bahar, "Attaining Optimal Deterrence at Sea: A Legal and Strategic
Theory for Naval Anti-Piracy Operations," *Vanderbilt Journal of Transnational
Law* 40, no. 1 (2007): 12.

2 History

1 Matthew Lee, "Clinton: Time to Seize Pirate Loot – Urges Diplomacy to
Douse Bandit Activities," CNN, 16 April 2009, www.nbcnewyork.com/
news/archive/NATLClinton-Piracy-is-a-Fire-Raging.html.

2 Bruce A. Elleman, Andrew Forbes, and David Rosenberg, *Piracy and Maritime Crime, Historical and Modern Case Studies* (Newport, R.I.: Naval War
College Press, 2010).

3 Philip DeSouza, *Piracy in the Graeco-Roman World* (New York: Cambridge
University Press, 2002), 15.

4 Angus Konstam, *Piracy: The Complete History* (Oxford: Osprey, 2008),
10–11.

5 Henry A. Ormerod, *Piracy in the Ancient World: An Essay in Mediterranean
History* (Baltimore, Md.: Johns Hopkins University Press, 1997), 68.

6 Ibid.

7 Ibid.

8 This tradition is still reflected in US law: "Whoever, being engaged in any
piratical cruise or enterprise, or being of the crew of any piratical vessel,
lands from such vessel and commits robbery on shore, is a pirate, and shall
be imprisoned for life," 18 U.S.C. § 1661.

9 "With respect to their towns, later on, at an era of increased facilities of
navigation and a greater supply of capital, we find the shores becoming the
site of walled towns, and the isthmuses being occupied for the purposes of
commerce and defence against a neighbour. But the old towns, on account
of the great prevalence of piracy, were built away from the sea, whether on
the islands or the continent, and still remain in their old sites. For the
pirates used to plunder one another, and indeed all coast populations,
whether seafaring or not," Thucydides, *History of the Peloponnesian War*,
Book 1, Richard Crawley, trans.

10 Adam J. Young, *Contemporary Maritime Piracy in Southeast Asia: History,
Causes, Remedies* (Singapore: Institute of Southeast Asian Studies, 2007).

11 Bjørn Møller, *Piracy, Maritime Terrorism and Naval Strategy* (Copenhagen:
Danish Institute for International Studies, 2008), 10. Møller claims that
"Her first measure was to grant letters of marque to privateers, authorising
them to plunder all whom they fell in with."

12 Jane Margaret Strickland, *Rome, Regal and Republican: A Family History
of Rome* (London: A. Hall, 1854), 290. This is based on an account by Pliny.

13 Plutarch, *The Parallel Lives* (London: Heinemann, 1917). Available at: http://
penelope.uchicago.edu/Thayer/E/Roman/Texts/Plutarch/Lives/Pompey*.html.

14 Konstam, *Piracy: The Complete History*, 20.
15 Ibid., 22.
16 Plutarch, *The Parallel Lives*.
17 Elleman, Forbes, and Rosenberg, *Piracy and Maritime Crime, Historical and Modern Case Studies*, 37
18 Lübeck, Rostock, and Wismar, "Proscribe Pirates," in *A Source Book for Medieval History*, eds. Oliver J. Thatcher and Edgar McNeal (New York: Scribners, 1905), 610–11. Available at: www.furthark.com/hanseati cleague/ src_pri_1259pirateprosc.shtml.
19 "Decrees of the Hanseatic League," in ibid., 612. Available at: www.fur thark.com/hanseaticleague/src_pri_1265decree.shtml.
20 O.M. Powers, *Commerce and Finance* (New York: Powers & Lyons, 1903), Chapter V available at http://chestofbooks.com/finance/economics/Com merce-and-Finance/Chapter-V-The-Cape-Route-To-India-Portuguese-Comme rce-Spa.html.
21 "Mediterranean 1550–1650: The Barbary Pirates," www.dieli.net/Sicily Page/MedTimeline/BarbaryPirates.html.
22 Robert Davis, *Christian Slaves, Muslim Masters: White Slavery in the Mediterranean, the Barbary Coast, and Italy, 1500–1800* (Hampshire: Palgrave Macmillan, 2004).
23 Charles Thomas-Stanford, *About Algeria; Algiers, Tlemçen, Constantine, Biskra, Timgad* (London: John Lane, 1912), 71. Available at: www.archive. org/details/aboutalgeriaalgi00thomuoft.
24 Frederic Chapin Lane, *Venice, a Maritime Republic* (Baltimore, Md.: Johns Hopkins University Press, 1973), 419.
25 Polyaenus, *Stratagems*, Book 8, ch. 53 (adapted from the English translation by R. Shepherd, 1793), available at www.attalus.org/translate/polyaenus 8B.html#53, 1.
26 John N.K. Mansell, *Flag State Responsibility* (Berlin: Springer-Verlag, 2009), 13.
27 Stephen M. Carmel, "The Big Myth of Somali Pirates," *Proceedings Magazine* 136, no. 12 (2010), www.usni.org/magazines/proceedings/2010– 12/big-myth-somali-pirates.
28 Michael B. Oren, "From the Shores of Tripoli to the Tigris," *New York Times*, 17 March 2008, www.nytimes.com/2008/03/17/opinion/17iht-edoren. 1.11186604.html.
29 Elizabeth R. DeSombre, "Convenient Fishing: Participation in International Fishery Management," paper for presentation at the International Studies Association Annual Meeting, March 2002, New Orleans, http:// isanet.ccit.arizona.edu/noarchive/desombre.html.
30 Ram Presh Anand, "'Tyranny' of the Freedom-of-the-Seas Doctrine," *International Studies* 12, no. 3 (1973): 416–29.
31 Kristin Eddy, "Even the Most Familiar Jar in the Spice Rack Holds a History of Piracy, Shipwreck, and Nation-Building," *Chicago Tribune*, 18 April 2001, http://articles.chicagotribune.com/2001–4–18/entertainment/ 0104180470_1_spices-cardamom-importer/2.
32 U.S. District Court, New Hampshire, "Federal Courts and the Admiralty Oar," www.nhd.uscourts.gov/ci/history/oar.asp.
33 This is the gist of Markham's comments as described by Douglass Burgess, Jr. in *The Pirates' Pact: The Secret Alliances between History's Most Notorious Buccaneers and Colonial America* (New York: McGraw-Hill, 2009), 156.

34 Barry Richard Burg, *Sodomy and the Pirate Tradition: English Sea Rovers in the Seventeenth Century Caribbean* (New York: New York University Press, 1995), 115.
35 Wombwell, *The Long War against Piracy: Historical Trends*, 12.
36 Marcus Rediker, *Villains of all Nations: Atlantic Pirates in the Golden Age* (Boston, Mass.: Beacon Press, 2004), 145.
37 It is interesting to note that many pirates turned to slave trading as a "legitimate business."
38 Piracy Act 1698 (repealed 5.11.1993), www.legislation.gov.uk/aep/Will3/11/7/contents. The first English law against piracy, the Offences at Sea Act of 1536 required trial in England.
39 Rediker, *Villains of all Nations: Atlantic Pirates in the Golden Age*, 127.
40 Ibid, 145.
41 Two women were sentenced to death as well. Anne Bonny and Mary Read are the legendary women who disguised themselves as men to join a pirate crew. Both women were pregnant upon receiving their death sentences and thus their lives were spared.
42 Robert Anthony, "Piracy in Early Modern China," *IIAS Newsletter*, no. 6 (2005), www.iias.nl/nl/36/IIAS_NL36_07.pdf.
43 Ibid.
44 Konstam, *Piracy: The Complete History*, 300.
45 Elleman, Forbes, and Rosenberg, *Piracy and Maritime Crime, Historical and Modern Case Studies*, 48.
46 Jack C. Ramsay, Jr., *Jean Laffite: Prince of Pirates* (Austin, Tex.: Eakin Press, 1996), 72.
47 The Internet Movie Database, "All-Time Box Office: World-Wide," www.imdb.com/boxoffice/alltimegross?region=world-wide.
48 Xan Rice and Abdiqani Hassan, "'We Consider Ourselves Heroes' – a Somali Pirate Speaks" *The Guardian*, 22 November 2008, www.guardian.co.uk/world/2008/nov/22/piracy-somalia.
49 Agence France-Presse, "Somali Parliament Blocks Piracy Bill," *Inquirer Global Nation*, 19 January 2011, http://globalnation.inquirer.net/news/breakingnews/view/20110119-315308/Somali-parliament-blocks-piracy-bill.
50 Alfred Rubin, *Law of Piracy* (Brill Academic Publishers, 1998), quoted in Rediker, *Villains of All Nations: Atlantic Pirates in the Golden Age*, 28.
51 "To Strengthen the Navy," *The New York Times*, 12 January 1890, http://query.nytimes.com/mem/archive-free/pdf?res=F70F11FD3F5F10738DDDA B0994D9405B8085F0D3.
52 Mansell, *Flag State Responsibility*.
53 Ibid.
54 *London Times* 1958, as quoted in Mansell, *Flag State Responsibility*, 98, fn. 20.
55 United Nations Conference on Trade and Development, *Review of Maritime Transport 2009* (Geneva: United Nations, 2009), 36.

3 The nuts and bolts of twenty-first century maritime governance relevant to combating piracy

1 Thanks to Jens Vestergaard Madsen for his research and writing assistance in this chapter.
2 Shabtai Rosenne, "The International Maritime Organization Interface with the Law of the Sea Convention," in *Current Maritime Issues and the*

International Maritime Organization, eds. Myron H. Nordquist and John Norton Moore (The Hague: Kluwer Law International, 1999), 251. Available at: http://books.google.com/books?id=XHK3-esL7akC&pg=PA29 1&dq=International+Maritime+Organization&client=firefox-a&source=gbs &_toc_r&cad=4#v=onepage&q&f=false.

3 IMO, "The History of IMO," http://www.imo.org/About/HistoryOfIMO/ Pages/Default.aspx.

4 See IMO, "Djibouti Code of Conduct," www.imo.org/OurWork/Security/ PIU/Pages/DCoC.aspx; "Train-the-Trainer," www.imo.org/OurWork/Securi ty/TC/Pages/Train-the-Trainer.aspx; and "Reports on Piracy and Armed Robbery," www.imo.org/OurWork/Security/PiracyArmedRobbery/Pages/Pir ateReports.aspx. See IMO, "SUA Treaties," www.imo.org/About/Conventio ns/ListOfCon ventions/Pages/SUA-Treaties.aspx; "International Convention for the Safety of Life at Sea (SOLAS), 1974," www.imo.org/About/Conven tions/ListOfConventions/Pages/International-Convention-for-the-Safety-of-L ife-at-Sea-(SOLAS),-1974.aspx; International Convention on Standards of Training, Certification and Watchkeeping for Seafarers (STCW), www.imo. org/About/Conventions/ListOfConventions/Pages/International-Convention-on-Standards-of-Training,-Certification-and-Watchkeeping-for-Seafarers-(ST CW). aspx; and "ISPS Code," www.imo.org/ourwork/security/instruments/ pages/ispscode.aspx.

5 Report of the Secretary-General on Possible Options to Further the Aim of Prosecuting and Imprisoning Persons Responsible for Acts of Piracy and Armed Robbery at Sea off the Coast of Somalia, Including, in Particular, Options for Creating Special Domestic Chambers Possibly with International Components, a Regional Tribunal or an International Tribunal and Corresponding Imprisonment Arrangements, Taking into Account the Work of the Contact Group on Piracy off the Coast of Somalia, the Existing Practice in Establishing International and Mixed Tribunals (Security Council document S/2010/394), 26 July 2010.

6 Report of the Special Adviser to the Secretary-General on Legal Issues Related to Piracy off the Coast of Somalia Summary: A Plan in 25 Proposals (Security Council document S/2011/30), 25 January 2011.

7 Bureau of Political-Military Affairs, Seventh Plenary Meeting of the Contact Group on Piracy off the Coast of Somalia, www.state.gov/t/pm/rls/othr/ misc/151795.htm.

8 6th Plenary Session of the Contact Group on Piracy off the Coast of Somalia, Final Communiqué, www.marad.dot.gov/documents/FINAL_ COMMUNIQUE-Sixth_Plenary_Meeting_6–10-10.pdf.

9 Contact Group on Piracy off the Coast of Somalia, Regional Counter-Piracy Capability Development Needs Assessment and Prioritisation Mission to East Africa and the Gulf of Aden, 20 October 2009, www.parliament.uk/ deposits/depositedpapers/2009/DEP2009–3000.pdf.

10 Ibid.

11 UNODC, "Counter-Piracy Programme: Support to the Trial and Related Treatment of Piracy Suspects," www.unodc.org/documents/easternafrica// piracy/20110209.UNODC_Counter_Piracy_February_Issue.pdf.

12 "UNDP in Somalia," www.so.undp.org/.

13 Report of the Secretary-General Pursuant to Security Council Resolution 1897 (2009) (Security Council document S/2010/556), 27 October 2010.

132   *Notes*

14 INTERPOL, www.interpol.int/.
15 INTERPOL, "UN Security Council Resolution Underscores Role of INTERPOL in Securing Maritime Piracy Prosecutions," www.interpol.int/Public/ICPO/PressReleases/PR2011/PR025.asp.
16 Council of the European Union, "Council Decision 2010/766/CFSP of 7 December 2010 amending Joint Action 2008/851/CFSP on a European Union Military Operation to Contribute to the Deterrence, Prevention and Repression of Acts of Piracy and Armed Robbery off the Somali Coast," *Official Journal of the European Union* L 327 (2010): 49–50. Available at: www.interpol.int/Public/ICPO/PressReleases/PR2010/PR107Decision.pdf.
17 INTERPOL, "INTERPOL European Commission-funded project to assist East African police fight maritime piracy," www.interpol.int/public/icpo/pressreleases/pr2011/pr013.asp; and "Maritime Piracy," www.interpol.int/Public/ICPO/FactSheets/DCO03.pdf.
18 Richard Meade, "Political Will on Piracy Yet to Bring Firm Action," *Lloyd's List*, 6 May 2011, www.lloydslist.com/ll/sector/regulation/article369860.ece.
19 For more information, see "ReCAAP Information Sharing Centre," www.recaap.org/Home.aspx.
20 The Contracting Parties to ReCAAP are: Bangladesh, Brunei, Cambodia, China, Denmark, India, Japan, South Korea, Laos, Myanmar, the Netherlands, Norway, the Philippines, Singapore, Sri Lanka, Thailand, and Vietnam. Press release, "The Fifth Governing Council Meeting of the ReCAAP Information Sharing Centre," www.recaap.org/Portals/0/docs/News%20and%20Press%20Releases/Press%20Release%20(2011-03-08).pdf. Notably neither Malaysia nor Indonesia have signed on although some cooperation between these countries and the ReCAAP Information Sharing Center does take place.
21 ReCAAP ISC, APEC/OPFR Workshop, "Measures for Combating Piracy and Armed Robbery against Ships in Asia," www.apec-tptwg.org.cn/new/Archives/tpt-wg32/Maritime/MAR-SEC/Mr.Teo.pdf.
22 Speech by Yoshiaki Ito, Executive Director of ReCAAP ISC, April 2007. See www.recaap.org/news/pdf/news/april07.pdf.
23 Gordon Corera, "Resurgence of Piracy on Tsunami-Hit Seas," The BBC, 11 May 2005, http://news.bbc.co.uk/2/hi/asia-pacific/4535677.stm.
24 Ian Storey, "Securing Southeast Asia's Sea Lanes: A Work in Progress," Asia Policy no. 6 (2008): 116. Available at: www.nbr.org/publications/asia_policy/Free/AP6/AP6_E_Storey.pdf.
25 Shicun Wu and Keyuan Zou, eds., *Maritime Security in the South China Sea: Regional Implications and International Cooperation* (Surrey, United Kingdom: Ashgate Publishing, 2009).
26 "Factsheet: Milestones of Malacca Strait Patrols," www.mindef.gov.sg/imindef/news_and_events/nr/2008/mar/28mar08_nr/28mar08_fs.html.
27 John Michael Lewis Geragotelis, Sea Piracy in Southeast Asia: Implications for Countering Maritime Terrorism in the United States (Monterey, Calif.: Naval Postgraduate School, 2006). Available at: http://edocs.nps.edu/npspubs/scholarly/theses/2006/Jun/06Jun_Geragotelis.pdf.
28 African Union, "African Maritime Transport Charter" (African Union document AU/MT/MIN/1), 16 October 2009. Available at: www.africa-union.org/root/ua/conferences/2010/avril/psc/07avril/African_Union_Member_S

tates_06–07_April_2010_Experts_Meeting_on_Maritime_Security_ and_Sa fety_Strategy-Documentation/African%20Maritime%20Transport%20Char ter%202009.doc.

29 African Union, "Durban Resolution on Maritime Safety, Maritime Security and Protection of the Marine Environment in Africa" (African Union document AU/MT/MIN/DRAFT/Res.), 16 October 2009. Available at: www.africa-union.org/root/ua/conferences/2010/avril/psc/07avril/African_Un ion_Member_States_06–07_April_2010_Experts_Meeting_on_Maritime_ Se curity_and_Safety_Strategy-Documentation/African%20Maritime%20Trans port%20Charter%20Durban%20Resolution.doc.

30 Africa's Integrated Maritime (AIM) Strategy is under development and not publicly available as of time of writing.

31 African Union, "Durban Resolution on Maritime Safety, Maritime Security and Protection of the Marine Environment in Africa."

32 The signatories are: Comoros, Djibouti, Egypt, Eritrea, Ethiopia, Jordan, Kenya, Madagascar, Maldives, Mauritius, Oman, Saudi Arabia, Seychelles, Somalia, Sudan, Tanzania, and Yemen. IMO, "Djibouti Code of Conduct," www.imo.org/OurWork/Security/PIU/Pages/DCoC.aspx.

33 Phil Holihead, "Djibouti Code of Conduct: Implementation Update," www.imo. org/OurWork/Security/PiracyArmedRobbery/Presentations_Piracy/IMO-PIU.pdf.

34 IMO, "Project Implementation Unit," www.imo.org/OurWork/Security/ PIU/Pages/Project-Implementation-Unit.aspx.

35 "Joint Communiqué from the Eastern and Southern Africa – Indian Ocean Ministers and European Union High Representative at the 2nd Regional Ministerial Meeting on Piracy and Maritime Security in the Eastern and Southern Africa and Indian Ocean Region," 7 October 2010.

36 Jim Garamone, "Roughead Urges More Naval Cooperation," American Forces Press Service, 7 October 2009, www.navy.mil/search/display.asp? story_id=48825.

37 Dorian Bakogiannis, *The Costs and Risks of Somali Piracy* (Washington, DC: Center for Advanced Defense Studies: Culture and Conflict Studies Program, April 2011).

38 Martin Murphy, *Somalia: The New Barbary? Piracy and Islam in the Horn of Africa* (New York: Columbia University Press, 2011), 131.

39 NATO Shipping Centre, "Counter Piracy Operation Ocean Shield," www. shipping.nato.int/CounterPir.

40 See EU NAVFOR Somalia, www.eunavfor.eu/.

41 The Maritime Security Centre – Horn of Africa website is located at: www. mschoa.org/Pages/default.aspx.

42 See: www.consilium.europa.eu/showpage.aspx?id=1870&lang=en.

43 US Naval Institute, Observing the Establishment of CTF-151, http://blog. usni.org/2009/01/09/observing-the-establishment-of-ctf-151/.

44 The UK Foreign & Commonwealth Office, "The International Response to Piracy," www.fco.gov.uk/en/global-issues/conflict-prevention/piracy/interna tional-response.

45 Bjoern H. Seibert, "Avoiding the Institutional 'Beauty Contest' in Countering Somalian Piracy," Royal United Services Institute, www.rusi.org/ analysis/commentary/ref:N494B76B8AC75E/.

46 Report of the Special Adviser to the Secretary-General on Legal Issues Related to Piracy off the Coast of Somalia, Summary: A Plan in 25

Proposals (Security Council document S/2011/30), 24 January 2011. Available at: http://oceansbeyondpiracy.org/documents/Somalia_S_2011_30.pdf.
47 International Chamber of Commerce, "International Maritime Bureau," www.icc-ccs.org/index.php?option=com_content&view=article&id=27:welco me-to-the-international-maritime-bureau&catid=25:home&Itemid=16.
48 Nautilus Institute, "Roots of Piracy in Southeast Asia," www.nautilus.org/ publications/essays/apsnet/policy-forum/2007/the-roots-of-piracy-in-southea st-asia; Idarat Maritime, "New Strategies and Ideas for Countering Piracy off Somalia: Piracy Prosecutions; Human Rights Issues," www.idar atmarit ime.com/wordpress/?p=261.
49 The International Transport Workers' Federation: www.itfglobal.org/about-us/ index.cfm.
50 Ibid.
51 BIMCO, "Piracy and Security," www.bimco.org/upload/emag/Reflections 2010/flash.html#/10/.
52 Oceans Beyond Piracy is a project of One Earth Future Foundation, which has also funded the research for this book. For more information please see their website: www.oceansbeyondpiracy.org.
53 Frank. G. Madsen, *Transnational Organized Crime* (London: Routledge, 2009), 30.
54 NATO Shipping Center, IMB Piracy Reporting Center, IMO, UKMTO, Djibouti Code, ReCAAP.

4 Evolving norms and conventions

1 Ram Prakash Anand, *Origin and Development of the Law of the Sea: History of International Law Revisited* (The Hague: Martinus Nijhoff Publishers, 1982), 203.
2 Richard J. Goldstone and Adam M. Smith, *International Judicial Institutions: The Architecture of International Justice at Home and Abroad* (London: Routledge, 2009), 12.
3 Ibid.
4 The development of high levels of foreign direct investment has made individual states' property rights regimes more of a global issue than at any time in the past. For example a foreigner's right to establish a company and own property are now legitimate subjects for treaties and multinational discussions.
5 James A. Wombwell, *The Long War Against Piracy: Historical Trends* (Fort Leavenworth, Kansas: Combat Studies Institute Press. US Army Combined Arms Center, 2010), 110. (Wombwell gives the dates for Hammurabi as 1948–1905 BC but 1795–1750 BCE is more widely used.) Available at: http://www.dtic.mil/cgi-bin/GetTRDoc?AD=ADA522959&Location=U2 &doc=GetTRDoc.pdf.
6 R. Benedict, "The Historical Position of the Rhodian Law," *Yale Law Journal* 18, no. 4 (1909): 223–42.
7 Sir John C. Dalrymple Hay, *The Suppression of Piracy in China*, Edward Stanford, London, 1889, 6. Available at: http://www.archive.org/stream/ suppressionpira00haygoog#page/n4/mode/2up.
8 Jack Lang, *Report of the Special Adviser to the Secretary-General on Legal Issues Related to Piracy off the Coast of Somalia Summary: A plan in 25 proposals*, UN Document S/2011/30, 11. Available online at: http://security

councilreport.org/aft/cf/%7B65BFCF9B-6D27-4E9C-8CD3-CF6E4FF96FF
9%7D/Somalia%20S%202011%2030.pdf.

9 Available online at: http://www.unhcr.org/refworld/country,,,RESOLUTION
,SOM,456d621e2,48464c622,0.html.

10 For Somalia, a count in February 2011 at: http://en.wikipedia.org/wiki/
List_of_diplomatic_missions_of_Somalia. Other sources give a low count
of 19 and a high of 24 for Somali embassies abroad. For Taiwan, author
count at: http://www.mofa.gov.tw/webapp/1p.asp?ctnode=1864&ctunit=30&
basedsd=30&mp=6.

11 George B. Davis, *The Elements of International Law: With an Account of its
Origin, Sources, and Historical Developments*, Harper & Brothers, New
York, 1900, 60.

12 Louis Fargo Brown, *The Freedom of the Seas* (New York: E.P. Dunton,
1919), 5.

13 James Boswell, *The Scots Magazine*. Vol 45, Murray and Cochran, Edinburgh,
1783. 452. (See fourth article of treaty.)

14 Lassa F.L. Oppenheim, *International Law: a Treatise, Volume 1* (New
York: Longmans, Green, and Company, 1920), 410

15 Grotius did not promote *mare liberum* as a principle but rather as a means
to break up Portuguese domination. Later, in 1613 when it suited his
interest he argued against *mare liberum* and in favor of Dutch domination
of trade near the Spice Islands. See The Straight Dope, *In International
Waters, Are You Beyond the Reach of the Law?* www.straightdope.com/col
umns/read/2250/in-international-waters-are-you-beyond-the-reach-of-the-law.

16 James A. Wombwell, *The Long War against Piracy: Historical Trends*, 110.
(Wombwell usees the date 1842. However Hay, *Op Cite* quotes an instruction
dated May 18th, 1844. "...It is my direction Her Majesty's ships and vessels, as
well as those of the Indian service employed on the coast of China, do not
interfere directly or indirectly with any ship, vessel, or boat, they may fall in with,
belonging to Chinese subjects, under the supposition that he may be a pirate, or
have been engaged in any unlawful act, unless he shall have within view attacked
some British vessel or subject..." It is not clear that there is a prior order.)

17 Joseph Walter Bingham, reporting, "Draft Convention on Piracy," *American
Journal of International Law* 26, Supplement (1932), 739–49.

18 Ibid., 764.

19 Ibid., 760.

20 Ibid.

21 See, Section 26(1) and Schedule 5. Available on line at: http://www.legislation.
gov.uk/ukpga/1997/28

22 United Nations, "The United Nations Convention on the Law of the Sea
(A Historical Perspective)," www.un.org/Depts/los/convention_agreements/
convention_historical_perspective.htm.

23 An impressive visualization of this is available on the National Oceanic &
Atmospheric Administration website, at http://aquaculture.noaa.gov/pdf/
20_eezmap.pdf.

24 United Nations, "The United Nations Convention on the Law of the Sea
(A Historical Perspective)."

25 Andrew Murdoch, "Conference Report: Overview of Legal Issues Relating
to Different Private Interests," *Africa Programme and International Law
Conference Report* (London: Chatham House, 2009).

26 Ibid.
27 Many thanks to Douglas Guilfoyle and Saoirse de Bont whose papers "Counter-Piracy Law Enforcement and Human Rights," *International & Comparative Law Quarterly* 59, no. 1 (2010), and *Prosecuting Pirates and Upholding Human Rights Law: Taking Perspective* (Louisville, Colo.: One Earth Future Foundation, 2010), informs much of our thinking on human rights law.
28 Thomas G. Weiss and Rorden Wilkinson, "Foreword," in *Contemporary Human Rights Ideas*, Bertrand G. Ramcharan (London: Routledge, 2008), xiv.
29 Bertrand G. Ramcharan, *Contemporary Human Rights Ideas* (London: Routledge, 2008), 160.
30 United Nations, "60th Anniversary: Universal Declaration of Human Rights," www.un.org/events/humanrights/udhr60/. It is important to note that although UDHR has strong moral authority it is a non-binding resolution of the General Assembly.
31 Wombwell, *The Long War against Piracy: Historical Trends, 155.*
32 Most of the world's states have ratified the ICCPR. A notable exception is China, which has signed the treaty but has not ratified it. The full list is available at http://treaties.un.org/Pages/ViewDetails.aspx?src=TREA TY&mtdsg_no=IV-4& chapter=4&lang=en.
33 All Council of Europe member states (this includes most of Europe) are party to the convention with the expectation that all will ratify it at their earliest convenience.
34 Some 77 states have ratified CAT. They include members of the EU, Australia, Canada, India, Russia, and the United States. Notably absent are countries such as Kenya, Japan, and the Seychelles which are parties to CAT but have not ratified. The full list is available at http://treaties.un.org/Pages/ViewDetails.aspx?src=TREATY&mtdsg_no=IV-9&chapter=4&lang=en.
35 Eugene Kontorovich, "'A Guantanamo on the Sea': The Difficulty of Prosecuting Pirates and Terrorists," *California Law Review* 98 (2010): 243–76.
36 Kontorovich, "'A Guantanamo on the Sea': The Difficulty of Prosecuting Pirates and Terrorists," 243–76.
37 International Covenant on Civil and Political Rights. Available at: http:// www2.ohchr.org/english/law/ccpr.htm.
38 Guilfoyle, "Counter-Piracy Law Enforcement and Human Rights," 159
39 Statements by Nicola Duckworth, director of the Europe and Central Asia Programme at Amnesty International, "UK's Highest Court to Hear Key Test Cases on Deportations with Assurances," www.amnesty.org/en/news-and-updates/news/uk-highest-court-hear-key-test-cases-deportations-assuran ces-20081022.
40 Guilfoyle, "Counter-Piracy Law Enforcement and Human Rights," 163.
41 Ibid.
42 Another reason for this reluctance has often been deficiency in developed countries' piracy laws. In Germany, courts may only exercise jurisdiction if German interests are attacked. Indeed, no cases have been brought before EU or US courts where there was no nexus of interests.
43 These rights are also spelled out in Articles 5 and 6 of the Convention for the Protection of Human Rights and Fundamental Freedoms. Available at: www.echr.coe.int/NR/rdonlyres/D5CC24A7-DC13–4318-B457–5C9014916D 7A/0/ENG_CONV.pdf.

44 International Covenant on Civil and Political Rights. Available at: http://
www2.ohchr.org/english/law/ccpr.htm.
45 Guilfoyle, "Counter-Piracy Law Enforcement and Human Rights," 163.
46 International Covenant on Civil and Political Rights. Available at: http://
www2.ohchr.org/english/law/ccpr.htm.
47 In one instance two Iraqis held prisoner by the United Kingdom,
al-Sadoon and Mufdhi, sought to prevent their transfer into Iraqi custody
claiming that this transfer would violate their rights under the ECHR.
A British court heard their case, which fulfilled the requirement of redress,
but ultimately ruled against them. See Nehal C. Bhuta, *Conflicting International
Obligations and the Risk of Torture and Unfair Trial: Critical
Comments on R (Al-Saadoon and Mufdhi) v Secretary of State for Defence;
Al-Sadoon and Mufdhi v United Kingdom*, www.gpia.info/files/u578/Bhuta_
final.pdf.
48 See, for example, Cordula Droege, "Transfer of Detainees: Legal Framework,
Non-Refoulement and Contemporary Challenges," *International
Review of the Red Cross*, 90 (2008): 669–701, which discusses the way that
non-refoulement as a legal principle remains binding on states and international
organizations in the case of prisoners of war, but also the way that
this principle has in practice been disregarded by some states.
49 Kontorovich, "'A Guantanamo on the Sea': The Difficulty of Prosecuting
Pirates and Terrorists," 246.
50 Thanks to Frank Madsen who introduced us to this idea in his book,
Transnational Organized Crime (London: Routledge, 2009).

5 Current debates

1 Bolton, John, "Treat Somali pirates like terrorists: Viewing sea raids as law
enforcement issue hasn't worked," *The Washington Times*, October 14th
2011. Available online at: www.washingtontimes.com/news/2011/oct/14/trea
t-somali-pirates-like-terrorists/.
2 International armed conflict is defined as armed conflict between states or
between a state and an armed group within and external to any one state.
3 Douglas Guilfoyle, "The Laws of War and the Fight against Somali
Piracy," *Melbourne Journal of International Law*, 11 (2010).
4 Ibid.
5 United Nations Security Council Resolution 1851, http://www.unhcr.org/
refworld/country,,,,SOM,456d621e2,4952044e2,0.html.
6 United Nations, Department of Public Information, "Security Council
Authorizes States to Use Land Based Operations in Somalia," www.un.org/
News/Press/docs/2008/sc9541.doc.htm.
7 Guilfoyle, "The Laws of War and the Fight against Somali Piracy."
8 Micah Zenko, "What's Behind Limited Military Force?" *Washington Post*,
16 November 2010, http://voices.washingtonpost.com/political-bookworm/
2010/11/whats_behind_limited_military.html.
9 Ibid.
10 Ibid.
11 Max Weber, "Science as Vocation," in *Max Weber's Complete Writings on
Academic and Political Vocations*, ed. John Dreijmanis (New York: Algora
Publishing, 2008), 43.

138   *Notes*

12 Note, however, that as discussed in Chapter 2 this was often most successful when coupled with a mechanism for reconciliation or pardon that would provide pirates with a way to reintegrate into society. The historical argument that military force alone was sufficient may be an oversimplification of what were often multi-track mechanisms for suppression.
13 Oded Löwenheim, *Predators and Parasites: Persistent Agents of Transnational Harm and Great Power Authority* (Ann Arbor, Mich.: University of Michigan Press, 2007), 1–3.
14 Benjamin J. Priester, "Who is a 'Terrorist'? Drawing the Line between Criminal Defendants and Military Enemies," FSU College of Law, Public Law Research Paper No. 264, August 24, 2007 (see fn 170). Available at: http://ssrn.com/abstract=1009845.
15 Byron York, "Dem senator opposes trying terrorists in civilian courts," *Washington Examiner*, 13 November 2009, http://washingtonexaminer.com/blogs/beltway-confidential/dem-senator-opposes-trying-terrorists-civilian-cou rts#ixzz1OWnZNnlI.
16 Priester, "Who is a 'Terrorist?'"
17 Bruce Hoffman, *Inside Terrorism* (New York: Columbia University Press, 2006), 2.
18 See Jack Gibbs, "Conceptualizations of terrorism," *American Sociological Review* 54 (1989).
19 United Nations Convention on the Law of the Sea, Part VII, available at: www.un.org/Depts/los/convention_agreements/texts/unclos/part7.htm.
20 See Sarah Childress, "Somali Group Targets US in 'Sea Jihad'," *Weekend Australian*, 11 September 2010.
21 See Childress, Sarah, "Somali Group targets US in 'Sea Jihad'," *Weekend Australian*, 11 September 2010.
22 Byrnes, Andrew (2002). *Apocalyptic Visions and the Law: The Legacy of September 11*. A professorial address by Andrew Byrnes at the ANU Law School for the Faculty's "Inaugural and Valedictory Lecture Series", May 30, 2002. Available online at: http://law.anu.edu.au/CIPL/StaffPapersTalks& Submissions/Byrnes30May02.pdf.
23 The Economist, *A battle on many fronts*, Oct 4, 2001. Available online at: http://www.economist.com/node/806317.
24 Douglas Guilfoyle, "Treaty Jurisdiction over Pirates: A Compilation of Legal Texts with Introductory Notes", available at: http://ucl.academia.edu/ DouglasGuilfoyle/Papers/116803/Treaty_Jurisdiction_over_Pirates_A_Comp ilation_of_Legal_Texts_with_Introductory_Notes.
25 Yvonne M. Dutton, "Pirates and Impunity: Is the Threat of Asylum Claims a Reason to Allow Pirates to Escape Justice?" *Fordham International Law Journal* 34, no. 2 (2011): 241.
26 Michael Beck Pemberton, *'Pirate Jurisdiction': Fact, Fiction, and Fragmentation in International Law* (Louisville, Col.: One Earth Future Foundation, 2010), 15.
27 Lawrence Azubuike, "International Law Regime Against Piracy," *Annual Survey of International and Comparative Law* 15, no. 1 (2009): 55.
28 SUA Convention Article 6, Paragraph 4.
29 SUA Convention Article 8, Paragraph 1.
30 There is one case, United States of America, Plaintiff-Appellee, v. Lei SHI, Defendant-Appellant, No. 06–10389, Argued and Submitted November 6,

2007-April 24, 2008, which involved a case of piracy on the high seas in which there was no nexus to the United States. The Supreme Court ruled that under the SUA the United States had jurisdiction because he was found in US territory and that his arrival in the United States did not have to be voluntary.

31 Thanks to Charles Nicholas for his research and writing on venues for prosecution of pirates.

32 The failure of many states' legislatures to enact anti-piracy laws—as requested by international treaties—makes domestic prosecutions challenging. If a state does not criminalize piracy in its domestic legal code, in essence giving itself jurisdiction over piracy, it is unable to hear piracy cases.

33 Yvonne M. Dutton, "Bringing Pirates to Justice: A Case for Including Piracy within the Jurisdiction of the International Criminal Court," *Chicago Journal of International Law* 11, no. 1 (2010): 223.

34 Report of the Special Advisor to the Secretary-General on Legal Issues Related to Piracy off the Coast of Somalia (Security Council document S/2011/30), 25 January 2011.

35 Committee on Legal Affairs and Human Rights, "The Necessity to Take Additional International Legal Steps to Deal with Sea Piracy," § 4.2 (Council of Europe document no. 12194), 2010.

36 Committee on Legal Affairs and Human Rights, "The Necessity to Take Additional International Legal Steps to Deal with Sea Piracy."

37 Ibid.

38 Azubuike, "International Law Regime Against Piracy," 52.

39 Yvonne M. Dutton, "Bringing Pirates to Justice: A Case for Including Piracy within the Jurisdiction of the International Criminal Court," *Chicago Journal of International Law* 11, no. 1 (2010): 223.

40 For more information, see Pemberton, *'Pirate Jurisdiction': Fact, Fiction, and Fragmentation in International Law.*

41 Larry J. Siegel, "Criminology" (CA: Wadsworth, Cengage Learning, 2012).

42 Data from Combined Maritime Forces (CMF), 7 percent unknown disposition and 2 percent killed, as seen in Andrew Murdoch, "Recent Legal Issues and Problems Relating to Acts of Piracy off Somalia," in *Selected Contemporary Issues in the Law of the Sea*, ed. Clive R. Symmons (Leiden: Brill/Martinus Nijhoff Publishers, forthcoming).

43 Report of the Special Adviser to the Secretary-General on Legal Issues Related to Piracy off the Coast of Somalia (Security Council document S/2011/30), 25 January 2011.

44 See, for example, J.L. Miller & Andy Anderson, "Updating the Deterrence Doctrine," *The Journal of Criminal Law and Criminology* 77, no. 2 (1986): 418–38.

45 Roger Middleton, *Piracy in Somalia: Threatening Global Trade, Feeding Local Wars* (London: Chatham House, 2008), 12.

46 James A. Wombwell, *The Long War against Piracy: Historical Trends* (Fort Leavenworth, Kan.: Combat Studies Institute Press, 2010), 110. Available at: www.dtic.mil/cgi-bin/GetTRDoc?AD=ADA522959&Location=U2&doc=GetTRDoc.pdf.

47 Bronwyn E. Bruton, *Somalia: A New Approach* (Washington, DC: Council on Foreign Relations, 2010), 4. Al-Shabab is an Islamist insurgent group which controls much of the southern and central portions of Somalia (as of summer 2010).

48 Ibid.

49 Bronwyn E. Bruton, *Somalia: A New Approach.*
50 Ibid.
51 Ibid.
52 Thanks to Mani Chandy for his research on arming merchant vessels and the paying of ransoms.
53 Peter Chalk, "Maritime Piracy: Reasons, Dangers," and Solutions, www.rand.org/pubs/testimonies/2009/RAND_CT317.pdf.
54 Christopher Torchia, "Shoot at the Pirates? West Weighs Arming Ships," *Yahoo News*, 13 August 2009, http://news.yahoo.com/s/ap_travel/20090814/ap_tr_ge/eu_guns_on_ships.
55 Alan Cowell, "Pirates Attack Maersk Alabama Again," *New York Times*, 18 November 2009.
56 Laura Spadanuta, "Private Security Counters Pirates", www.securitymanagement.com/article/private-security-counters-pirates-005439.
57 Keith Bradsher, "Captain's Rescue Revives Debate Over Arming Crews," New York Times, 12 April 2009.
58 Associated Press, "Why No Guns? Owners Debate Arming Ships against Pirates," www.komonews.com/news/national/42801962.html.
59 John S. Burnett, *Dangerous Waters: Modern Piracy on the High Seas* (New York: Plume, 2003), 115.
60 Alan Cowell, "In First, Private Guards Kill Somali Pirate," *New York Times*, 24 March 2010.
61 Scott Carney, "An Economic Analysis of the Somali Pirate Business Model," *Wired Magazine* 17, no. 7 (2009).
62 Jerry Frank, "Ransom for Seafarers Could Rocket to $50m," Lloyd's List, 15 September 2008, www.lloydslist.com/ll/sector/Insurance/article44463.ece. Also referenced in Marts, Piracy Ransoms—Conflicting Perspectives.
63 Anna Bowden, One Earth Future, "The Economic Cost of Maritime Piracy" (December 2010), http://oceansbeyondpiracy.org/documents/The_Economic_Cost_of_Piracy_Full_Report.pdf.
64 Charles Marts, *Piracy Ransoms—Conflicting Perspectives* (Louisville, Col.: One Earth Future Foundation, 2010).
65 "Somali Pirates Get Ransom, Free Ship but Keep Indian Hostages," MSNBC, 15 April 2011.
66 Ibid.
67 Thanks to Divya Sama for her research and writing on the geopolitical concerns of counterpiracy.
68 Caroline Vavro, "Piracy, Terrorism, and the Balance of Power in the Malacca Strait," Canadian Naval Review 4, no. 1 (2008): 13.
69 Vavro, "Piracy, Terrorism, and the Balance of Power in the Malacca Strait."
70 Peter J. Brown, "China's Navy Sails Past India's Dock," *Asia Times Online*, 22 October 2009, www.atimes.com/atimes/China/KJ22Ad02.html.
71 US Energy Information Administration, "International Energy Outlook 2010 – Highlights," www.eia.doe.gov/oiaf/ieo/highlights.html.
72 Robert D. Kaplan, "Center Stage for the 21st Century," *Foreign Affairs*, March/April 2009. Available at: www.foreignaffairs.com/articles/64832/robert-d-kaplan/center-stage-for-the-21st-century.
73 "Jane's Sentinel Security Assessment, Northeast, Navy, China," http://search.janes.com/Search/documentView.do?docId=/content1/janesdata/sent/cnasu/chins130.htm@current&pageSelected=allJanes&keyword=Navy%2C

%20China&backPath=http://search.janes.com/Search&Prod_Name=CNAS
&#toclink-j1131124871777438.

74 Peter Apps, "More than Piracy Drives Naval Build-Up," *Washington Post*, 24 October 2010.

6 Key gaps and criticisms

1 Tom Maliti, "Piracy off Somalia's Coast Increases," Associated Press, 17 October 2007, www.hiiraan.com/comments2-news-2007-oct-piracy_off_ som alia_s_coast_increases.aspx.

2 According to Martin Murphy, "[t]here are few international observers who study the problem in detail who now doubt that political figures in Puntland, despite all the denials that have been issued and the obfuscation that has gone on, have, at the very least, a substantial influence over pirate activity." Martin N. Murphy, "Dire Straits: Taking on Somali Pirates," *World Affairs* (July/August 2010). Available at: www.worldaffairsjournal. org/articles/2010-JulyAugust/full-Murphy-JA-2010.html.

3 Open registries started in the 1930's as a way for American cruise ships to avoid prohibition, but became more popular as a way to avoid registration in belligerent or occupied states during the Second World War and later was used to reduce operating costs and taxes.

4 Kearsarge Amphibious Ready Group transited the Suez Canal on 2 March 2011 in order to support NATO operations off the coast of Libya.

5 "Hostage Captain Rescued; Navy Snipers Kill 3 Pirates," CNN World, 12 April 2009, http://articles.cnn.com/2009-04-12/world/somalia.pirates_1_navy-snipers-three-pirates-bill-gortney?_s=PM:WORLD.

6 Declaration on the Inadmissibility of Intervention and Interference in the Internal Affairs of State adopted at the 91st Plenary Meeting, 9 December 1981, Art. II(b) (UN General Assembly document A/RES/36/103), 9 December 1981.

7 United Nations Convention on the Law of the Sea, Part VII High Seas, art. 100.

8 Ibid., art. 113.

9 Lawrence Azubuike, "International Law Regime against Piracy," *Annual Survey of International & Comparative Law* 15, no. 1 (2010).

10 Robin Geiss and Anna Petrig, *Piracy and Armed Robbery at Sea: The Legal Framework for Counter-Piracy Operations in Somalia and the Gulf of Aden* (New York: Oxford University Press, 2011), 40.

11 Ibid.

12 Ibid.

13 Ibid.

14 There are exceptions to this idea. China, for instance, does not have any laws addressing piracy or even an actual term for "piracy," yet because it has ratified both UNCLOS and SUA it abides by their guidelines and has tried and convicted pirates based on them. See Zou Keyuan, "Seeking Effectiveness for the Crackdown of Piracy at Sea," *Journal of International Affairs* 59, no. 1 (2005).

15 Efthimios E. Mitropoulos, secretary-general of the IMO at the Athena 09 Crisis Management International Conference. Athens, Greece, 30 September– 3 October 2009.

16 Jose Luis Jesus, "Foreword," *American University Law Review* 59, no. 5 (2010): 1,213–1,217.

17 There is another criticism to which the authors do not adhere; namely, that UNCLOS is too limited because it defines piracy as acts committed solely for private ends, thereby excluding acts of terrorism from its purview. We agree with UNCLOS's inclusion of a private ends requirement in its definition of piracy.

18 Article 103 defines a pirate ship as one that is "intended by the persons in dominant control to be used for the purpose of committing one of the acts referred to in article 101." UNCLOS, art. 103 (Definition of a pirate ship or aircraft).

19 Eugene Kontorovich, *Equipment Articles for the Prosecution of Maritime Piracy* (Louisville, Col.: One Earth Future Foundation, 2010).

20 IMO, *Status of Multilateral Conventions and Instruments in Respect of Which the International Maritime Organization or its Secretary General Performs Depositary or Other Functions as at 28 February 2011* (London: International Maritime Organization, 2011), 393.

21 IMO, "Status of Conventions Summary 5 March 2011," www.imo.org/About/Conventions/StatusOfConventions/Pages/Default.aspx.

22 Richard Meade, "Political Will on Piracy Yet to Bring Firm Action," *Lloyd's List*, 6 May 2011, www.lloydslist.com/ll/sector/regulation/article369860.ece.

23 John Mo, "Options to Combat Maritime Piracy in Southeast Asia," *Ocean Development & International Law* 33 (2002): 343–58, 350–51.

24 Mo, "Options to Combat Maritime Piracy in Southeast Asia," 351.

25 Ibid., 352.

26 Murphy, "Dire Straits: Taking on Somali Pirates," World Affairs.

27 Fareed Zakaria, "The Failed-State Conundrum," Washington Post, 19 July 2010, www.washingtonpost.com/wp-dyn/content/article/2010/07/18/AR2010071802734.html.

28 Ibid.

29 Bronwyn E. Bruton, *Somalia: A New Approach.* (Washington, DC: Council on Foreign Relations, 2010), 4.

30 Nigerian constitution Chapter VI, Part I, Sect 162.

31 Michael Logan, "25 Police Cars in Europe," *Somalia Report*, 22 April 2011, www.somaliareport.com/index.php/post/586/25_Police_Cars_in_Europe?PHPSESSID=43a52238944ce31e4aa8d8a80e325e00.

32 "No Stopping Them: For All the Efforts to Combat it, Somali Piracy is Posing an Ever Greater Threat to the World's Shipping," *The Economist*, 3 February 2011. Available at: www.economist.com/node/18061574.

33 Azubuike, "International Law Regime Against Piracy," 56.

34 Ibid.

35 UNCLOS Annex VI, art. 1, para. 2.

36 Murphy, "Dire Straits: Taking on Somali Pirates."

7 Emerging trends and future directions

1 Markus Junianto Sihaloho, "Indonesian Military Went After Somali Pirates, Killed 4," *Jakarta Globe*, 2 May 2011, www.thejakartaglobe.com/indonesia/indonesian-military-went-after-somali-pirates-killed-4/438633.

2 Ben Arnoldy, "India pushes back on Somali pirates' new 'mother ship' offensive," *Christian Science Monitor*, 7 February 2011, www.csmonitor.com/World/Asia-South-Central/2011/0207/India-pushes-back-on-Somali-pirates-new-mother-ship-offensive.

3 "The Somali Pirates Are Getting Smarter and More Aggressive," *Business Insider*, 31 January 2011, www.businessinsider.com/the-somali-pirates-are-getting-smarter-and-more-aggressive-2011-1#ixzz1IxyWahRG.

4 Anna Bowden. "The Economic Cost of Piracy," One Earth Future working paper, December 2010, http://oceansbeyondpiracy.org/cost-of-piracy/economic.

5 Kaija Hurlburt, Eamon Aloyo, Jon Huggins, Jens Madsen, Kasey Pennington, Maisie Pigeon, and D. Conor Seyle, "The Human Cost of Somali Piracy," Oceans Beyond Piracy working paper, http://oceansbeyondpiracy.org/cost-of-piracy/human-cost-somali-piracy.

6 Contact Group on Piracy off the Coast of Somalia, Report of Working Group 3, 28 February 2011, www.cusnc.navy.mil/marlo/WG3%20final%20report%2028%20feb%2011.pdf.

7 Daniel Howden, "Somali pirates are 'using torture' as defense shield," *The Independent*, 3 February 2011, www.independent.co.uk/news/world/africa/somali-pirates-are-using-torture-as-defence-shield-2202614.html.

8 Sihaloho, "Indonesian Military Went After Somali Pirates, Killed 4."

9 As quoted in "New Call for Armed Guards on Ships in Pirate Waters," *IFW*, 23 March 2011, www.ifw-net.com/freightpubs/ifw/article.htm?artid=20017859075&src=rss.

10 EUNAVFOR, "Pirate Dies in Attempted Hijacking – EU NAVFOR Detains Pirate Action Group," 24 March 2010, www.eunavfor.eu/2010/03/pirate-dies-in-attempted-hijacking-%E2%80%93-eu-navfor-detains-pirate-action-group/.

11 For more information, see the UNODC website on piracy at: www.unodc.org/easternafrica/en/piracy/index.html.

12 Martin Murphy and Joseph Saba, "Countering Piracy: The Potential for Onshore Development," in *Global Challenge, Regional Response: Forging a Common Approach to Maritime Piracy* (Dubai: Dubai School of Government, 2011).

13 Bronwyn E. Bruton, "In the Quicksands of Somalia: Where Doing Less Helps More," *Foreign Affairs*, November/December 2009.

14 Matteo Crippa, http://www.faceofshipping.com/, *Following Security Council Debate, UN Deploys Assessment Mission to West Africa*, See http://www.intermanager.org/forums/topic/following-security-council-debate-un-deploys-assessment-mission-to-west-africa

15 Cahal Milmo, "Insurance Firms Plan Private Navy to Take on Somali Pirates," *The Independent*, 28 September 2010, www.independent.co.uk/news/world/africa/insurance-firms-plan-private-navy-to-take-on-somali-pirates-2091298.html.

16 Security Association for the Maritime Industry, brief, www.marsecreview.com/wp-content/uploads/2011/04/SAMI-Brief-3-Apr-11.pdf.

17 Judith Swan, "Fishing Vessels Operating Under Open Registers and the Exercise of Flag State Responsibilities," FAO Fisheries Circular No. 980, FIPL/C980, Food and Agriculture Organization of the United Nations, Appendix 9, tbl. 3. This paper shows that in 2002 the top 21 FOCs collected about $63 million in registration fees.

18 Kearsarge Amphibious Ready Group transited the Suez Canal on 2 March 2011.

19 "Germany Calls for International Court to Prosecute Piracy," *Fox News*, 23 December 2008, www.foxnews.com/story/0,2933,471804,00.html.

144 *Notes*

20 "Piracy—Best Practice Being Ignored." *Tanker Operator*, 11 March 2011, www.tankeroperator.com/news/todisplaynews.asp?NewsID=2602.
21 In the interests of full disclosure, it should be noted that the writing of this book was supported by the One Earth Future Foundation.
22 United Nations Conference on Trade and Development (UNCTAD), *Review of Maritime Transport 2009* (New York: United Nations, 2009), 36.

Select bibliography

1. Henry A. Ormerod, *Piracy in the Ancient World* (Baltimore, MD: Johns Hopkins University Press, 1996) gives the reader first-person accounts of ancient piracy. It proved invaluable in understanding ancient views of what constituted piracy and how widespread was the practice.
2. Angus Konstam, *Piracy: The Complete History* (Oxford: Osprey, 2008) gives a helpful overview of piracy to those who may be familiar only with piracy of the Golden Age. Through writing that is both engaging and highly informative, Konstam shows the reader that piracy has been a fact of life from the earliest times until the present.
3. Marcus Rediker, *Villains of All Nations: Atlantic Pirates in the Golden Age* (Boston: Beacon Press, 2004) reads more like a novel than a history textbook. Rediker's scholarship along with the vivid portrayal of the life (and death) of eighteenth-century pirates make this book an invaluable aid to learning about golden age piracy.
4. Peter Lehr, ed., *Violence at Sea: Piracy in the Age of Global Terrorism* (New York: Routledge, 2007) offers many useful chapters on a wide array of topics from a critique of UNCLOS to a discussion on the convergence of piracy and terrorism. This edited book is especially useful in that it brings together many of the key thinkers and policymakers who are confronting the challenges posed by piracy. It is also useful in that its focus is on Southeast Asian piracy while so many texts concentrate on Somali-based piracy.
5. R. P. Anand, *Origin and Development of the Law of the Sea* (Springer, 1982) offers a history of international law from an Asian perspective showing the influence of Asian thinking on European creation of international law. When so much thinking on the emergence of international maritime law focuses on the influence of Europe and specifically England, this book gives a vital, alternative perspective.
6. Adam J. Young, *Contemporary Maritime Piracy in Southeast Asia: History, Causes and Remedies* (Singapore: Institute of Southeast Asian Studies, 2007) is one of a handful of modern piracy books dealing with Southeast Asian piracy. Adam Young's definition of piracy, in particular,

proved useful in our thinking on this perplexing, yet fundamental question, "what is piracy?"

7. Eugene Kontorovich, "The Piracy Analogy: Modern Universal Jurisdiction's Hollow Foundation," *Harvard International Law Journal* 45, no. 1 (Winter 2004): 183–237 introduces a controversial idea, namely that universal jurisdiction for piracy is wrong. Much of the piracy arrests and prosecutions are based on the idea that any state can claim jurisdiction for piracy on the high seas even if they have no nexus to the piratical act. If universal jurisdiction for piracy was no longer available it would make arresting suspected pirates much more difficult.

8. The Oceans Beyond Piracy website (http://oceansbeyondpiracy.org) is an invaluable source for current counterpiracy operations. It contains an interactive timeline of events related to piracy and several useful studies.

9. Douglas Guilfoyle's "Counter-Piracy Law Enforcement and Human Rights," *International and Comparative Law Quarterly*, 59 (2010): 141–169 explains how human rights laws have informed current counterpiracy operations.

10. Bronwyn E. Bruton, "Somalia, A New Approach," Council on Foreign Relations Center for Preventive Action, Council Special Report No. 52, March 2010, offers a unique, counter-intuitive perspective on how countries might help Somalis stabilize their country. Bruton travels regularly to Somalia and is therefore intimately familiar with this region. This first-hand knowledge is indispensable for a region in which most outsiders are reluctant to travel.

11. Roger Middleton, "Piracy in Somalia: Threatening Global Trade, Feeding Local Wars," Chatham House briefing paper, Africa Programme, October 2008 explores modern Somali piracy. Middleton is a researcher at Chatham House who, like Bronwyn Bruton, travels regularly to Somalia. He offers useful information on the pirates—where they live, how they operate, and how their activities affect ordinary Somalis.

12. Somalia Report (SomaliaReport.com) is a non-partisan website created in 2011 by Robert Pelton. It teams Western and Somali journalists to cover the daily news in Somalia. It covers piracy—and a host of other issues for anyone wanting to better understand the situation in Somalia—that are not covered by news outlets throughout the world.

13. The IMB website www.icc-ccs.org: the IMB is one of the main sources for data on piracy worldwide. It produces exhaustive quarterly reports that break out aspects of piracy into many useful categories, such as nationality of hijacked seafarers and sort of abuse they have suffered.

14. Martin N. Murphy, *Somalia: The New Barbary? Piracy and Islam in the Horn of Africa* (Hurst, 2010), is a detailed account of the forces at work which make Somali piracy so virulent. Information on Somalia is difficult to come by as it is considered one of the world's most dangerous places. Murphy has managed to compile vital information that we have not been able to find elsewhere.

Index